30p

D0767192

ESSENTIAL
BRITTANY

Original text by Lindsay Hunt
Revised and updated by Victoria Trott

© AA Media Limited 2010
First published 2008. Revised 2010.

ISBN 978-0-7495-6671-5

Published by AA Publishing, a trading name of AA Media Limited, whose registered
office is Fanum House, Basing View, Basingstoke, Hampshire RG21 4EA.
Registered number 06112600.

A CIP catalogue record for this book is available from the British Library

Colour separation by AA Digital Department
Printed and bound in Italy by Printer Trento S.r.l.

A04192
Maps in this title produced from mapping © MAIRDUMONT / Falk Verlag 2010
with updates from mapping © ISTITUTO GEOGRAFICO DE AGOSTINI S.p.A.,
NOVARA 2009

About this book

This book is divided into five sections.

The essence of Brittany pages 6–19
Introduction; Features; Food and drink; Short break

Planning pages 20–33
Before you go; Getting there; Getting around; Being there

Best places to see pages 34–55
The unmissable highlights of any visit to Brittany

Best things to do pages 56–73
Good places to have lunch; Top activities; Best beaches; Places to take the children and more

Exploring pages 74–185
The best places to visit in Brittany, organized by area

Maps
All map references are to the maps on the covers. For example, Dinan has the reference ✚ 13C – indicating the grid square in which it is to be found

Admission prices
Inexpensive (under €4)
Moderate (€4–€7)
Expensive (over €7)

Hotel prices
Prices are per double room per night:
€ budget (under €75); €€ moderate (€75–€120); €€€ expensive (over €120)

Restaurant prices
Prices are for a three-course meal per person without drinks:
€ budget (under €25); €€ moderate (€25–€60); €€€ expensive (over €60)

Contents

BEST THINGS TO DO

56 – 73

EXPLORING...

74 – 185

The essence of...

Brittany is the Gallic equivalent of Wales, Scotland or Ireland – France's very own Celtic nation. Its unique heritage is evident all around but especially in the west, where Breton culture (dance, folk music, language, games and traditional costumes) is celebrated at festivals throughout the year. Brittany is the land of *Argoat* (inland), once covered in dense forest, and *Armor*, France's longest regional coastline; a land of corsairs and record-breaking sailors, explorers and fishermen. And then there are the islands, each with its own distinct character, like wind-swept Ouessant or beautiful Belle-Île.

features

Brittany offers visitors far more than its magnificent coastline. Once covered in dense forest, the village-dotted interior has medieval castles, manor houses, historic churches and those uniquely Breton architectural treasures – parish closes.

GEOGRAPHY

● France's longest regional coastline: 1,800km (1,120 miles).

● Europe's highest tides: the difference between high and low tide in the Bay of St-Michel is 16m (52ft).

● 600km (370 miles) of navigable waterways.

● 5,000km (3,110 miles) of bridleways and footpaths, including the GR34 *sentier des douaniers* (Custom Man's Path) that stretches right around the coast.

● Two Regional Parks: Armorique – 172,000ha

(425,010 acres) of land and ocean, including the Monts d'Arrée, the Crozon peninsula and the islands of Ouessant and Sein; La Brière – 40,000ha (98,840 acres) of peatmarsh once submerged below the sea.

● Regions: Haute-Bretagne (Upper Brittany near the eastern Marches) and Basse-Bretagne (Lower Brittany to the west).

● Highest altitude: 384m/1,260ft (Tuchen Gador, Monts d'Arrée).

ADMINISTRATION

● Since 1973, the *département* of Loire-Atlantique has officially formed part of the Pays-de-la-Loire region, but culturally still considers itself to be Breton.

● The other four *départements* are Ille-et-Vilaine, Côtes d'Armor, Finistère and Morbihan.

ECONOMY

● About 60 per cent of Brittany's land is under cultivation, and is one of France's most productive agricultural regions.

● Dairy, poultry and pig-farming are important, but Brittany is especially renowned for market garden produce (artichokes, potatoes, cabbages, cauliflowers, peas, beans, salad crops, apples, strawberries etc).

● Despite dwindling fish stocks and EU quota systems, the fishing industry is a vital mainstay of Breton ports like Le Guilvinec, Douarnenez, Concarneau and Audierne.

● Tourism is one of the biggest earners. Brittany is France's fourth most popular holiday area.

● Car manufacture and light engineering (electronics, computing, telecommunications) now supersede Brittany's declining shipbuilding and steel industries.

food & drink

Brittany produces a wide range of high-quality foodstuffs. Regional dishes make good use of seafood, pork and vegetables, but Bretons have a sweet tooth too, and love puddings and biscuits. Filled pancakes are a ubiquitous speciality.

SEAFOOD

Brittany is one of France's foremost fishing regions, and its seafood is superb. Visit a *criée* (fish auction) or fish farm for some idea of this marine cornucopoia. If you don't enjoy seafood much, you may be unable to look another *assiette de fruits de mer* in the eye by the end of your visit. These platefuls of seaweed and crushed ice, piled high with curious sea-creatures, can be a daunting sight. Most include mussels or oysters (prime local products). Crayfish, clams, crabs and scallops also put in an appearance.

If you prefer your fish hot, try a traditional Breton *cotriade*, or fish stew, somewhat less spicy than a *bouillabaisse*. Look out for freshwater species, especially in the Brière region. *Brochet beurre blanc* is a classic pike dish in Nantais white butter sauce. Most Breton of all is the lobster, often prepared in a sauce of tomatoes, garlic, shallots and cognac *(homard à l'armoricaine)*. On many menus it appears as *homard à l'américaine*, often attributed to a spelling mistake in a Parisian restaurant.

MEAT AND POULTRY

Steak Chateaubriand is the most widely known Breton meat dish. But Brittany is more famous for its dairy produce than its beef. More typical meat products include the distinctively flavoured *pré salé* (salt meadow) lambs raised on the salt marshes of Ouessant and Mont-St-Michel. *Gigot à la bretonne* (roast leg of lamb with haricot beans) is a local speciality.

Brittany produces vast quantities of pork, and *charcuterie* takes many forms – especially sausages, black puddings and *andouille*, a sort of pork haggis not to everyone's taste. Hearty peasant soups and casseroles like *kig ha farz* often contain ham or bacon. Some of France's most succulent chickens come from around Rennes, while the *challan* is a delicious duck from the Nantes region.

PANCAKES

Once, pancakes were a staple diet in Brittany, replacing bread in poor homes. You will find *crêperies* everywhere – a cheap, quick and filling way of satisfying hunger pangs, and a good choice for vegetarians. Pancakes are cheap when eaten standing up at a pancake stall – great for the entertainment value of watching them being made. The variety of fillings offered is imaginative, but the more exotic the filling, the more it will cost.

Two kinds are made: *crêpes* and *galettes*. Generally, *crêpes* are made with a wheat-flour batter and have sweet fillings. The more traditional *galettes* are made with heavier buckwheat flour and are generally savoury. You can buy them ready-made in packets or tins, though they are much nicer warm and fresh. *Crêpes dentelles* are paper-thin, lacy pancakes, a speciality of Quimper.

CAKES AND PUDDINGS

Like many Breton dishes, desserts tend to be very rich and heavy. One famous local cake is *far breton*, a flan based on eggs and milk with prunes or raisins. *Kouign amann* is a delicious and fattening pastry of sugar, butter and almonds. *Galettes de*

Pont-Aven (not to be confused with pancakes) are buttery biscuits similar to shortbread.

DRINKS

Brittany produces little wine, apart from Loire-Atlantique's Muscadet (which now officially belongs to the Pays de la Loire region). The local tipples are cider *(cidre)* or barley beer *(cervoise)*. Tastings are offered all over the region in cider museums or breweries. Stronger applejack potions are also on sale. *Pommeau* is a local apéritif. *Lambig* is the Breton equivalent of the Norman *calvados*, though quite hard to track down. Another local drink is *chouchen*, a honey-based mead. A sparkling variety is also made.

short break

If you only have a short time to visit Brittany and would like to take home some unforgettable memories, you can do something local and capture the real flavour of the area. The following will give you a wide range of sights and experiences that won't take long, won't cost very much and will make your visit very special.

- **Eat pancakes.** A savoury *galette* (made with buckwheat flour) followed by a sweet *crêpe* makes a quick, inexpensive, filling meal. You'll find *crêperies* all over Brittany – look for the *crêperie gourmande* quality label.

- **Visit some parish closes.** These unique sights (elaborately carved, walled religious complexes) are mostly clustered around the Armorique Regional Park. They date from the 16th and 17th centuries when new-found prosperity was lavished on village churches.

- **Order an *assiette de fruits de mer.*** Whether oysters, scallops, mussels or langoustines are your favoured seafood, don't leave Brittany without trying one of these awesome platters, often served on beds of seaweed with big chunks of lemon.

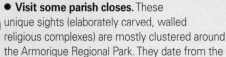

● **Head for the coastal extremities.** Brittany's westerly capes (Crozon, Sizun and Penmarc'h) and islands are especially dramatic during a gale, but the scenery is always stunning, especially along the old coastal watchpath *(sentiers des douaniers)* GR34.

● **Track down some megaliths.** Carnac has the best-known concentration of standing stones in Brittany, but dolmens, menhirs and cairns are sprinkled all over the region in quiet fields.

● **Experience a *criée*.** Brittany's bustling fish auctions can be visited in a number of ports – but you'll have to get up early to see anything happening. Ask the local tourist office.

● **Take a boat trip.** Brittany is perfect for boating and there's a wonderful choice of river cruises, island hops and trips along the inland waterways. Take your camera and binoculars to watch birds and seals.

● **Look out for festivals.** Most communities hold a festival or two during the year. Some are major cultural events attracting visitors from far and wide, but village saints' days and *pardons* can be just as memorable and often more genuinely typical of Breton life.

● **Try a typical Breton cake or pudding.** A *kouign amann* (a sugary almond cake) or *far breton* (an eggy flan with prunes or raisins) will stoke up your energy levels. Local *pâtisseries* and specialist shops sell a bewildering variety of Breton biscuits too (packed in attractive tins, they make great presents to take home).

● **Test the beaches.** Whatever else you do in Brittany, spend time on its glorious beaches. Scrubbed clean by the highest tides in Europe, many have EU Blue Flag status. Some are dangerous – heed flags and warning signs.

Planning

Before you go

WHEN TO GO

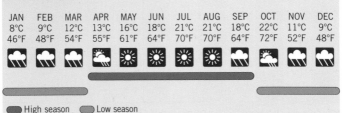

JAN	FEB	MAR	APR	MAY	JUN	JUL	AUG	SEP	OCT	NOV	DEC
8°C	9°C	12°C	13°C	16°C	18°C	21°C	21°C	18°C	22°C	11°C	9°C
46°F	48°F	54°F	55°F	61°F	64°F	70°F	70°F	64°F	72°F	52°F	48°F

● High season ● Low season

Brittany has a mild maritime climate with few extremes of temperature, but the weather is always unpredictable, and can change rapidly. Be prepared for rain at any time of year. The hilly inland areas are often wetter than the low-lying coastal regions, and have wider temperature fluctuations. The wettest months are usually in autumn and winter, but snow and frost are rare and generally short-lived. Average summer daytime temperatures are around 20°C (68°F) and highest in August. The south coast is warmer and quite a bit sunnier than the Channel coast, and some areas are mild enough for vines and subtropical plants to flourish. Coastal regions are usually tempered by sea breezes, which can reach storm force from time to time.

WHAT YOU NEED

● Required
○ Suggested
▲ Not required

Some countries require a passport to remain valid for a minimum period (usually at least six months) beyond the date of entry – contact their consulate or embassy or your travel agency for details.

	UK	Germany	USA	Netherlands	Spain
Passport	●	●	●	●	●
Visa (regulations can change—check before booking your journey)	▲	▲	▲	▲	▲
Onward or Return Ticket	▲	▲	▲	▲	▲
Health Inoculations	▲	▲	▲	▲	▲
Health Documentation (► 23, Health Insurance)	▲	▲	▲	▲	▲
Travel Insurance	○	○	○	○	○
Driving Licence (National or International)	●	●	●	●	●
Car Registration Document (if own car)	●	●	●	●	●

WEBSITES

www.bretagne35.com
www.brittany-best-breaks.com
www.brittanytourism.com
www.cotesdarmor.com

www.finisteretourisme.com
www.loire-atlantique-tourisme.com
www.morbihan.com
www.tastybrittany.com

TOURIST OFFICES AT HOME

In the UK

Atout France
Lincoln House, 300 High Holborn
London WC1V 7JH
☏ 09068 244 123 (60p per minute)

In the USA

Atout France
825 Third Avenue (29th Floor)

New York NY 10022
☏ 514/288-1904

Atout France
9454 Wilshire Boulevard
Suite 210
Beverly Hills CA 90212
☏ 310/271-6665

HEALTH INSURANCE

Nationals of EU and certain other countries can get medical treatment in France at reduced cost on production of a European Health Insurance Card (EHIC), although private medical insurance is still advised and is essential for all other visitors.

As for general medical treatment (see above), nationals of EU countries can obtain dental treatment at reduced cost. About 70 per cent of a dentist's standard fee can be refunded. Private medical insurance is still advisable for all.

TIME DIFFERENCES

GMT	France	Germany	USA (NY)	Netherlands	Spain
12 noon	1PM	1PM	7AM	1PM	1PM

France is on Central European Time, one hour ahead of Greenwich Mean Time (GMT +1), but from late March, when the clocks are put forward one hour, until late October, French summer time (GMT +2) operates.

NATIONAL HOLIDAYS

1 Jan *New Year's Day*
Mar/Apr *Easter Sunday and Monday*
1 May *Labour Day*
8 May *VE Day*

May Ascension Day
May/Jun *Whit Sunday and Monday*
14 Jul *Bastille Day*
15 Aug *Assumption Day*

1 Nov *All Saints' Day*
11 Nov *Remembrance Day*
25 Dec *Christmas Day*

WHAT'S ON WHEN

Most of Brittany's festivals and cultural events take place in the short tourist season between Easter and October. Precise dates may change from year to year. Annually updated events listings are available from regional and local tourist offices.

April

Erquy, Loguivy, St-Quay-Portrieux: *Fête des Coquilles* (two days of scallop celebrations with tastings and live music)
www.erquy-tourisme.com
Nantes: *Carnival* www.nantes-tourisme.com

May

Binic: *Fête de la Morue* (four days of maritime activities and fun) www.ville-binic.fr
St-Brieuc: *Art Rock Festival* (four days of concerts and art exhibitions) www.artrock.org
Tréguier: *Pardon de St Yves* (► 72)

June

Le Faouët: *Pardon de Ste-Barbe*
St-Jean-du-Doigt: *Pardon de St-Jean-du-Doigt*

July

Carhaix: *Les Vieilles Charrues* (France's largest music festival) www.vieillescharrues-asso.fr
Dinan: *Fête des Remparts* (► 73)
Fouesnant: *Fête des Pommiers* (traditional music, dance and tastings to celebrate cider)
www.tourisme-fouesnant.fr
Gourin: *Fête de la Crêpe* (two days of music, dance and tastings)

Locquirec: *Pardon de St-Jacques* (sea festival)

Locronan: *Petites/Grandes Troménies* (▶ 72)

Pont l'Abbé: *Fête des Brodeuses* (Breton music, dance and costumes over four days) www.ot-pontlabbe29.fr

Quimper: *Festival de Cornouaille* (▶ 73)

Rennes: *Les Tombées de la Nuit* (▶ 73)

Ste-Anne-d'Auray: *Grand Pardon* www.sainte-anne-auray.com

Vannes: *Jazz à Vannes* (open-air festival) www.mairie-vannes.fr

August

Concarneau: *Fête des Filets Bleus* (▶ 73)

Guingamp: *Festival St Loup* (dance festival) www.dansebretonne.com

Île de Fedrun: *Fête de la Brière* (two days of rural activities) www.parc-naturel-briere.fr

Paimpol: *Fête du Chant Marin* (three-day festival of sea shanties, world music and a gathering of 300 sailboats. Next one in 2011) www.paimpol-goelo.com

Lorient: *Festival InterCeltique* (▶ 73)

Perros-Guirec: *Festival de la Cité des Hortensias* (three days of modern Celtic music in the open air) http://hortensias-gwalarn.org

Quimper: *Semaines Musicales* (three weeks of baroque, classical and contemporary music) www.semaines-musicales-quimper.org

Roscoff: *Fête de l'Oignon Rose* (weekend of onion-themed celebrations) www.roscoff-tourisme.com

Ste-Anne-la-Palud: *Pardon* (▶ 72)

St-Malo: *La Route du Rock* (three-day pop, rock and dance music festival) www.laroutedurock.com

September

Camaret-sur-Mer: *Pardon and Blessing of the Sea* (▶ 72)

Lamballe: *Mille Sabots* (celebration of Breton horse breeds) www.mille-sabots.fr

Le Folgoet: *Grand Pardon* (▶ 72)

Quiberon: *Festival de la Gastronomie Bretonne* (food tastings and competitions) www.quiberon.com

October

Dinard: *British Film Festival* (celebration of old and new British films) www.festivaldufilm-dinard.com

Nantes: *Celtomania* (month-long Celtic festival) www.celtomania.fr

Getting there

BY AIR

Rennes Airport

6km (4 miles) to city centre

N/A

10 minutes

10 minutes

Nantes Airport

12km (7.5 miles) to city centre

N/A

20 minutes

15 minutes

Budget airlines Ryanair (www.ryanair.com) and Flybe (www.flybe.com) operate direct flights to Dinard, Brest, Nantes and Rennes from various UK and Irish airports. British Airways (www.ba.com) and Air France (www.airfrance.com) fly directly to Nantes from London. If you fly to Paris, you can pick up an internal flight with Air France or Brit Air (Air France's Morlaix-based subsidiary, www.britair.com) to several Breton towns, including Lannion, Lorient and Quimper, or continue by rail or rental car.

BY RAIL

You can travel from London's St Pancras International terminal to Paris by Eurostar train via the Channel Tunnel in just over two hours. Services are frequent and generally efficient and comfortable. The quickest way to reach Brittany is to leave the train at Lille and board a high-speed TGV Atlantique Ouest connection. This saves the bother and expense of changing stations in Paris (from Gare du Nord to Gare Montparnasse).

You can book Eurostar tickets and any connecting services through Rail Europe (www.raileurope.co.uk for the UK; www.raileurope.com and www.eurail.com for the US). The further ahead you can book, the cheaper the fare is likely to be. On-line reservations may be cheaper still, and include no booking fees. Rail passes may be worth considering, but must be booked in advance. Brittany's rail network is fairly limited and not practical for extensive touring.

BY FERRY

To reach Brittany from the UK, you can take a direct ferry route to a Breton port, or take a short Channel crossing followed by a longish overland haul through northwestern France. The longer sea crossings are obviously more expensive, and possibly uncomfortable in rough weather, but whichever route you choose, overall journey time and costs are unlikely to differ greatly. If you take a short crossing, your choice of operators is between P&O Ferries (www.poferries.com) and Sea France (www.seafrance.com), which operate on the Dover–Calais route, or Eurotunnel, which operates the rapid-transit shuttle service through the Channel Tunnel (www.eurotunnel.com).

The longer routes across the western Channel are run mainly by Brittany Ferries (www.brittanyferries.com), which operates to St-Malo (from Portsmouth) and to Roscoff (from Plymouth). Services from Ireland are run by Irish Ferries (www.irishferries.com), which operates to Roscoff from Rosslare, and Brittany Ferries (from Cork to Roscoff). Condor Ferries (www.condorferries.co.uk) operates fast-craft summer services to St-Malo from Poole and Weymouth via the Channel Islands.

If you're heading for eastern Brittany it is also worth considering the shorter sea crossings to Normandy, though these generally cost much the same as the Breton ones. Brittany Ferries, Condor Ferries and Irish Ferries run crossings to Cherbourg and Caen.

Getting around

PUBLIC TRANSPORT

Internal flights Regular flights from Paris and other French cities with Air France to Nantes, Rennes, Brest, Lannion, Lorient, Quimper (just over 1 hour). BritAir (subsidiary of Air France) operates daily flights between Nantes and Brest. Finis'Air connects Brest and the Île d'Ouessant.

Trains Fast TGV trains connect Paris with Nantes, Rennes, Lorient, Quimper and Brest. Within Brittany, SNCF rail lines run from Rennes along the north and south coasts, but there are few cross-country routes.

Buses All major towns have a bus station *(gare routière)*, but the bus network is fragmented and many different companies operate. The coast has more regular routes than the interior. Some services run in conjunction with the railway (SNCF). Many timetables are designed to serve the needs of commuters and schoolchildren; services are dramatically reduced at weekends.

Boats and ferries A large number of operators serve Brittany's offshore islands, including Belle-Île, Île de Batz, Ouessant, Bréhat and Groix.

Urban transport Major centres have urban bus services. Rennes has a limited metro service, mainly used by commuters. Nantes has an extensive, well-integrated and very efficient mass transit network, including trams. Tourist passes are available.

TAXIS

Taxis are a costlier option than public transport. They pick up at taxi ranks *(stations de taxi),* found at railway stations and airports. Hotels and restaurants can usually give a taxi call number. Check the taxi has a meter; there is a pick-up charge plus a rate per minute.

FARES AND TICKETS

Students/youths Students can obtain discounts on transport, admission prices, entertainment and so forth with an International Student Identity Card. If you are under 26 but not a student, an International Youth Travel Card or a European Youth Card (Euro 26 card) can obtain many similar discounts. Visit www.istc.org for details.

Senior citizens A Carte Senior gives discounts of up to 50 per cent on rail transport for the over-60s. It costs €56, but is valid for a year (www.senior-sncf.com). If you have your passport, you may get a discount.

DRIVING

- The French drive on the right side of the road.
- Seat belts must be worn in front seats at all times and in rear seats where fitted. Children under 10 must travel in the rear unless there are no rear seats or they are already occupied by children under 10.
- Random breath-testing takes place. Never drive under the influence of alcohol.
- Fuel, including unleaded *(sans plomb)* and diesel *(gazole)* is widely available. Fuel stations are numerous along main roads but rarer in rural areas. Some on minor roads are closed on Sundays. Maps showing petrol stations are available from main tourist offices.
- Speed limits on toll motorways *(autoroutes)*: 130kph/80mph (110kph/68mph when wet); non-toll motorways and dual carriageways: 110kph/68mph (100kph/62mph when wet). In fog (visibility less than 50m/55yds): 50kph/31mph all roads
  Country roads: 90kph/56mph (80kph/50mph when wet)
  Urban roads: 50kp/31mph (limit starts at town sign)
- It is compulsory to carry a reflective jacket and a warning triangle in your car. Place the triangle 30m/33yds behind the car in the event of an accident or breakdown. On motorways ring from emergency phones (every 2km/1.2 miles) to contact the breakdown service.

CAR RENTAL

All airports and most major railway stations have car rental offices. Pre-booked car rental packages organized by tour operators, airlines, ferry operators or French Railways (SNCF) may be cheaper than renting locally.

Being there

TOURIST OFFICES
Comité Régional du Tourisme de Bretagne
1 rue Raoul Ponchon
35069 Rennes
☎ 02 99 36 15 15

Comité Départemental de Tourisme d'Ille-et-Vilaine
5 rue du Pré Botté
35101 Rennes Cedex 3
☎ 02 99 78 47 47

Departmental Tourist Offices
Comité Départemental de Tourisme de Finistère
4 rue du 19 Mars 1942
29018 Quimper Cedex
☎ 02 98 76 20 70

Comité Départemental de Tourisme de Côtes d'Amor
7 rue St-Benoît, 22046 St-Brieuc
☎ 02 96 62 72 00

Comité Départemental de Tourisme de Loire-Atlantique
11 rue du Château de L'Eraudière
44306 Nantes Cedex
☎ 02 51 72 95 40

Comité Départemental de Tourisme de Morbihan
PIBS allée Nicolas Leblanc
56010 Vannes
☎ 0825 135 656

MONEY
The euro (€) is the official currency of France. Banknotes are in denominations of €5, €10, €20, €50, €100, €200 and €500, and coins in denominations of 1, 2, 5, 10, 20 and 50 cents, and €1 and €2. Traveller's cheques can be changed at most banks, but take some cash. Visa/Barclaycard (Carte Bleue) and MasterCard/Access (Eurocard) are widely accepted in hotels, restaurants and major stores.

TIPS/GRATUITIES

Yes ✓ No ✗		
Restaurants/cafes/bars (service included, tip optional)	✗	
Taxis	✓	€1–€1.50
Chambermaids/Porters	✓	€1–€2
Tour guides	✓	€1–€1.50
Toilet attendants	✓	small change

POSTAL SERVICES

Post offices *(bureaux de poste)* are well signed, and generally open Mon–Fri 8–5, Sat 8–noon. In smaller places, opening hours may be shorter and offices may close for lunch. Main post offices sometimes stay open until later in the evenings. Postboxes are yellow.

TELEPHONES

Telephone numbers in France comprise ten digits; the first two numbers for Brittany are 02 (omit 0 if dialling from the UK). Nearly all public phones use prepaid cards now *(télécartes)*. Some cards give cheaper overseas calls than standard *télécartes*, so ask before you buy if you need to phone abroad. Dial the international code if you're phoning abroad with a mobile.

International dialling codes

From France:

UK: 00 44

Germany: 00 49

USA and Canada: 00 1

Netherlands: 00 31

Spain: 00 34

Emergency telephone numbers

Police: 17

Fire: 18

Ambulance: 15

General emergency number: 112

EMBASSIES AND CONSULATES

UK ☎ 01 44 51 31 00

Germany ☎ 01 53 83 45 00

USA ☎ 01 43 12 22 22

Netherlands ☎ 01 40 62 33 00

Spain ☎ 01 44 43 18 00

HEALTH ADVICE

Sun advice The sunniest (and hottest) months are July and August, but the good weather can start in June and continue to October. Generally, the weather is relatively mild, though take care on the beach and when walking. Drink plenty of fluids, wear a hat and make sure you apply a good sunscreen.

Drugs Pharmacies – recognized by their green cross sign – have qualified staff able to offer medical advice, provide first aid and prescribe and provide a wide range of drugs, though some are available by prescription *(ordonnance)* only.

Safe water It is safe to drink tap water served in hotels and restaurants, but never drink from a tap marked *eau non potable* (not drinking water). Bottled water is cheap and widely available.

PERSONAL SAFETY

The *Police Municipale* (blue uniforms) carry out police duties in cities and towns. The *Gendarmes* (blue trousers, black jackets, white belts), the national police force, cover the countryside and smaller places. The *CRS* deal with emergencies and riots. To avoid danger or theft:

- Do not use unmanned roadside rest areas at night.
- Cars, especially foreign cars, should be secured.
- In crowded places, beware of pickpockets.
- Police assistance: ☎ 17 from any call box.

ELECTRICITY

The French power supply is 220 volts. Type of socket: round two-hole sockets taking two-round-pin (or occasionally three-round-pin) plugs. British visitors should bring an adaptor; US visitors a voltage transformer.

OPENING HOURS

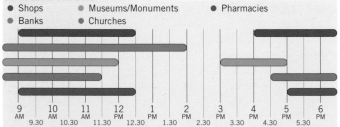

In addition to the times shown above, afternoon times of shops in summer can extend in the most popular centres. Most shops close Sunday and many on Monday. Small food shops open 7am and may open Sunday morning. Large department stores do not close for lunch and hypermarkets open 10am to 9 or 10pm, but may shut Monday morning. Banks are closed Sunday, as well as Saturday or Monday. Museums and monuments have extended summer hours. Many close one day a week: either Monday (municipal) or Tuesday (national).

LANGUAGE

French is the native language. English is spoken widely, especially in tourist areas and the larger and most popular centres; in smaller, rural places fewer people speak English. Attempts to speak French, or at least greet others in French, will be much appreciated. Below is a list of helpful words. More coverage can be found in the AA's *Essential French Phrase Book*.

hotel	l'hôtel	reservation	la réservation
guest house	chambre d'hôte	rate	tarif
room	la chambre	breakfast	le petit déjeuner
single room	une personne	toilet	les toilettes
double room	deux personnes	bathroom	la salle de bain
per person	par personne	shower	la douche
per room	par chambre	balcony	le balcon
one/two nights	une/deux nuits	key	la clef/clé
bank	la banque	banknote	le billet
exchange office	le bureau de change	coin	la pièce
post office	la poste	credit card	la carte de crédit
cashier	le caissier	traveller's cheque	le chèque de voyage
foreign exchange	le change extérieur	exchange rate	le taux de change
English pound	la livre sterling		
restaurant/cafe	la restaurant/le café	starter	le hors d'œuvre
table	la table	main course	le plat principal
menu	le menu	dish of the day	le plat du jour
set menu	le menu du jour	dessert	le dessert
wine list	la carte des vins	drink	la boisson
lunch/dinner	le déjeuner/le dîner	the bill	l'addition
yes/no	oui/non	yesterday	hier
please/thank you	s'il vous plaît/merci	how much?	combien?
hello /goodbye	bonjour/au revoir	expensive	cher
goodnight	bonsoir	open/closed	ouvert/fermé
sorry/excuse me	pardon/excusez-moi	you're welcome	de rien
help!	au secours!	okay	d'accord
today/tomorrow	aujourd'hui/demain	I don't know	je ne sais pas

Best places to see

1 Carnac

www.ot-carnac.fr

An extraordinary array of megaliths continues to baffle and fascinate experts and visitors alike.

It is not so much the town, a pleasant seaside resort, but the astonishing megaliths on its northern outskirts that attract interest in Carnac. Thousands head here to see them every year.

A good starting point for learning more about Brittany's megaliths is the **Musée de Préhistoire** on Carnac's main square. This gives a scholarly and rather technical presentation on local antiquities and archaeological theories (ask for the English translation notes). There are three main groups of *alignements* (rows of standing stones or menhirs): Ménec, Kermario and Kerlescan, containing some 2,700 stones altogether. You can see them from the roadside, but raised viewing platforms give a clearer idea of the patterns.

An information centre called **La Maison des Mégalithes** near the Alignements du Menec shows a video in French explaining the megaliths.

Other types of megalith can be found in and around Carnac, including dolmens (roofed table-like structures), tumuli (cairns) and gallery graves *(allées couvertes)*. These are less mysterious in that they were all presumably used as burial places. The megalith complex at nearby Locmariaquer (➤ 172) can be visited on a joint ticket with Carnac.

✚ 20H 🚌 Quiberon, Auray, Vannes; local shuttle TATOOVU and *petit train* (tourist train) serve *alignements* in high season

🛈 Place de L'Église, Carnac-Ville, 02 97 52 13 52

Musée de Préhistoire

✉ 10 place de la Chapelle ☎ 02 97 52 22 04; www.museedecarnac.com 🕐 Jul, Aug daily 10–6; Apr–Jun, Sep 10–12:30, 2–6 (closed Tue except holidays); Oct–Mar Wed–Mon 10–12:30, 2–5 ✋ Moderate 🍽 Crêperie Chez Marie (€), place de L'Église, 02 97 52 07 93

La Maison des Mégalithes

✉ Route des Alignements ☎ 02 97 52 29 81 🕐 Jul, Aug daily 9–8; May, Jun 9–7; Sep–Apr 10–5 ✋ Free; guided visits: moderate

2 Cathédrale St-Pierre, Nantes

Soaring vaults of bright stone give a lasting sense of space and light inside this impressive cathedral in the upper town.

Undaunted by its proximity to the formidable Château des Ducs de Bretagne (▶ 158, 159), Nantes' cathedral is built of clear, white tufa – quite a contrast to the sombre, weather-worn granite found in most Breton churches. Building work on St-Pierre began in 1434, on the site of an earlier Romanesque building, but it wasn't completed for another four and a half centuries. The towers were added in 1508. For all that, it seems a surprisingly coherent piece of Gothic workmanship, and post-war restoration work has given it a spruce and cared-for look. Its history, however, has been anything but tranquil. In 1800 a massive ammunition explosion in the nearby castle shattered all its precious 15th-century stained glass. During the Revolution, it served as a barn; it was bombed during World War II, and damaged by a fire in 1971, after which its interior had to be completely cleaned yet again. Today, it is light, airy and spacious.

The replacement windows in the choir (with over 500sq m (5,380sq ft) of modern stained glass) took over 12 years to create, and these alone justify a visit. St-Pierre's other main highlight is the magnificent Renaissance tomb of François II, the last Duke of Brittany, sculpted by the master-craftsman Michel Colombe between 1502 and 1507. The two main effigies depict François and his wife Margaret (parents of the Duchess Anne), and the corner statues are personifications of Justice, Fortitude, Temperance and Prudence. This elaborate tomb was commissioned by Anne in memory of her parents, and she asked that her heart be placed in it after her own death. Her wish was granted, though the heart vanished at some point during the Revolution. Another noteworthy 19th-century tomb commemorates General Lamoricière, famed for his adventures in Algeria.

🕆 26L ✉ Place St-Pierre 🕐 Apr–Oct daily 8–7; Sep–Mar 8–6 (except during Mass) 👃 Free 🍴 Brasserie F (€–€€), 4 place St-Pierre, 02 40 47 79 69

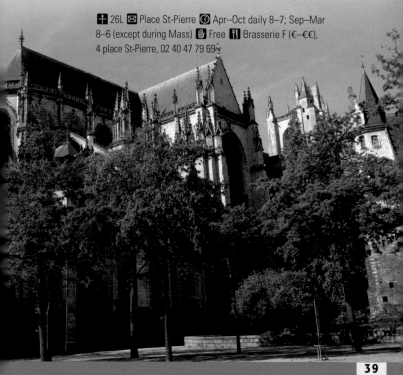

3 Château, Fougères

www.ot-fougeres.fr

The dominant feature of this shoe-making town on the Breton borderlands is a magnificent fortress, built to deter French encroachments from the east.

Built piecemeal from around 1166 until the 15th century, this mighty stronghold of schist and granite is one of the largest and best-preserved examples of medieval fortification in France. Its various sections demonstrate the advances in warfare that took place during the Middle Ages. Unusually, it is set *below* the town rather than above it, but on what was believed to be an easily defensible site – a tight loop in the River Nançon flanked by steep cliffs. The castle consists of a series of concentric enclosures protected by massive curtain walls studded with 13 towers, and encircled by a moat of weirs and waterfalls. The structure is in excellent condition, its machicolations and loopholes intact. Despite its impregnable appearance, however, it was repeatedly attacked and captured by Du Guesclin (➤ 44) and others, sometimes by stealth rather than force.

The castle made a romantic backdrop to Balzac's novel *Les Chouans* (1829), which describes the anti-Republican uprising in vividly gory detail.

Access for today's visitors leads via a bridge over the Nançon from a picturesque old quarter of tanneries and timbered houses near St-Sulpice church. The castle towers are beautifully reflected in the waters of the moat.

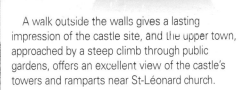

A walk outside the walls gives a lasting impression of the castle site, and the upper town, approached by a steep climb through public gardens, offers an excellent view of the castle's towers and ramparts near St-Léonard church.

✚ 16D ✉ Place Pierre-Simon ☎ 02 99 99 79 59
🕐 Jul–Aug daily 10–7; May, Jun, Sep Tue–Sun 10–1, 2–7; Oct–Apr Tue–Sun 10–12:30, 2–5:30; closed Jan
✋ Expensive 🍴 Crêperie Tivabro (€), place Marchix, 02 99 17 20 90 🚌 Lines 9 (Rennes), 14 (Vitré), 17 (St-Malo)
🛈 2 rue Nationale, 02 99 94 12 20

4 Côte de Granit Rose

www.perros-guirec.com

Bizarrely shaped rocks in improbable colours make the coastline around the popular resort of Perros-Guirec one of the most memorable scenes in Brittany.

This eye-catching 20km (12.5-mile) stretch of coast takes its name from the vividly coloured rocks mainly between Perros-Guirec and Trébeurden. Dramatic rocks begin at the Île de Bréhat, particularly noticeable at low tide when many reefs are exposed. But the small resorts of Ploumanac'h and Trégastel-Plage, further west, are the best places to see this russet rockery at its most striking, especially at sunset, when the stones take on an even fiercer glow. Not just the colours, but the weird forms they assume are remarkable. The best way to see them is on foot. The *sentier des douaniers* (watchpath) leading around the cliffs from Perros-Guirec through the Parc Municipal to the Pointe de Ploumanac'h is one of the most enjoyable walks in Brittany (➤ 114–115), leading past a grand jumble of rounded boulders weathered into strange organic-looking shapes, given

fanciful names like the Tortoise, the Pancakes and Napoleon's Hat.

The local rock is widely used as a building material, and when cut and polished, it sparkles beautifully and makes a most elegant finish (popular for Parisian shopfronts and luxury bathrooms). Similarly eroded rocks occur on other parts of the Breton coast, but nothing matches the warm rosy tints of the Pink Granite Coast.

The region around Perros-Guirec is one of Brittany's most popular tourist areas, with excellent facilities for family holidays. Inland, just to the west of Ploumanac'h, the Traouïéro valleys (Grand and Petit) offer wonderland walks along wooded creeks fringed by a chaos of huge and precariously balanced granite blocks. One valley contains an ancient tidal flour mill, in use until the 20th century.

➕ 8A 🖐 Free; guided walks inexpensive 🍴 Au Bon Accueil (€–€€), 11 rue Landerval, Perros-Guirec; 02 96 23 25 77 🚌 Line 15 from Lannion 🚢 Excursions to Les Sept Îles (➤ 113) from Perros-Guirec ℹ️ Maison du Littoral, Sentier des Douaniers (opposite Ploumanac'h lighthouse), 02 96 91 62 77 (exhibition, guided walks)

5 Dinan

www.dinan-tourisme.com

This picturesque medieval town of winding streets and timber-framed buildings overlooking the Rance makes a charming base for a night or two.

Standing high above the Rance estuary at what was for many centuries the lowest bridging point, Dinan was a strategic junction even in Roman times. By the 10th century it had an important Benedictine monastery, and by the 12th it was protected by high ramparts. The warrior knight of the Hundred Years War, Bertrand Du Guesclin, was born near the town in 1320. The large, tree-lined main square is named after him and has an equestrian statue of the hero. The weekly market is held here on Thursday; at other times the square makes a useful parking area. The Fête des Remparts, a biennial medieval fair, recreates Dinan's feudal heyday in a colourful pageant.

The château makes a good starting point, with a museum of local history in the machicolated keep. The 18th-century Gothic-Romanesque basilica of St-Sauveur is the last resting place of Du Guesclin's heart. Dinan's other main church is St-Malo, best seen from the grounds of the

Ancien Couvent des Cordeliers (a former Franciscan monastery). Many quaint buildings with sagging timbers and porticoes can be seen in the old streets. Climb the Tour de l'Horloge (clock tower) for a good town view.

The steep street winding down to the port is lined with picturesque, timbered merchant houses. Some now contain craft studios or shops. Terrace restaurants and cafes overlook the Rance from the quaysides. Discover all about the Rance at **La Maison de la Rance,** through models and displays inside and the flora and fauna of the marshlands reconstructed outside.

✚ 13C 🍴 Auberge du Pélican (€–€€), 3 rue Haute Voie, 02 96 39 47 05 🚌 7A Rennes and Dinard, 10 St-Malo 🚢 River trips or boat hire from the port; the Rance links with Brittany's major inland waterways
ℹ 9 rue du Château, 02 96 87 69 76
La Maison de la Rance
✉ Port de Dinan ☎ 02 96 87 00 40
🕐 Jul, Aug daily 10–7; Apr–Jun, Sep, Oct Tue–Sun 2–6; Nov–Mar Sun 2–6 ✋ Inexpensive

6 Guimiliau

One of the star examples of Finistère's *enclos paroissiaux*, Guimiliau's decorated calvary is a tour-de-force of 16th-century religious art.

Brittany's parish closes are unique to the region, and one of its greatest treasures. Most lie in or near the Parc Naturel Régional d'Armorique, and several of the best, including Guimiliau, are close together in the Élorn Valley near Landerneau.

The phrase *enclos paroissial* refers to the walled plot of hallowed ground around a church. Parish closes are used as graveyards, but their main interest lies in their architectural features. Typically, these consist of a triumphal gateway through

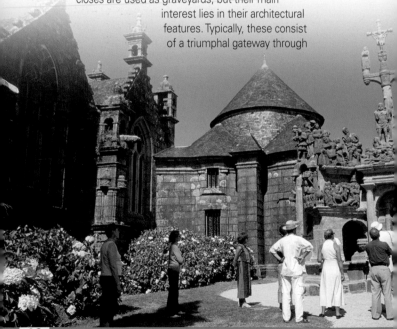

which funeral processions pass, an ossuary or charnel house (used for exhumed bones) and a sculpted granite calvary depicting mostly biblical scenes. The figures are generally portrayed in contemporary Renaissance dress, so they look like something from a Shakespearean play. Today the granite carvings are weather-worn and blotched with lichen, but still remarkable for their energy and detail.

The great era of the parish close was during the 16th and 17th centuries, when communities grew rich on sea trade and linen cloth. Their wealth was used to glorify God in religious art and architecture. Guimiliau has a vast, ornate calvary, one of the largest in the area, with over 200 separate figures over an arched base, including the Virgin, St Peter, St John and St Yves with Christ. Look for a horrific scene showing a young girl being torn apart by demons. This is Catell Gollet, whose downfall came when she stole consecrated wafers for her handsome lover (the Devil in disguise). The church interior is crammed with decoration, including wonderful woodwork and a 17th-century organ.

➕ 5C 🍴 Ar Chupen (€), 43 rue du Calvaire (a *crêperie* near the church)
✋ Free
❓ Guided tours in Jul and Aug
🚩 Place de la Mairie, 02 98 68 75 34

7 Océanopolis, Brest

www.oceanopolis.com

Brest's ambitious aquarium explores many aspects of the sea and the life within it, both off the Breton coast and worldwide.

This huge futuristic complex down by the docks is a major regional attraction in any terms. You could easily spend the best part of a day exploring its many exhibits relating to the seas and marine life of Brittany and other parts of the world. Expansion has resulted in a tripartite exhibition zone of pavilions linked by covered walkways. It has 50 separate aquariums, some containing up to a million litres of water.

The Temperate Pavilion concentrates on the Breton coastal waters and the Finistère fishing industry. Its huge tanks hold a massive number of local marine species, with special emphasis on those of economic importance (seaweeds, edible fish etc). There is also a seal tank, an

oceanography exhibition, a jellyfish collection and a tank where you can touch sea life such as starfish and sea urchins. The Tropical Pavilion has a shark tank and a colourful array of coral-reef fish, all in beautifully realistic settings. A diver feeds the fish, and a tropical greenhouse simulates a mangrove swamp. The Polar Pavilion has a tank of endearingly comical penguins (strategically placed windows show how they chug through the water). Other species from chillier climes seem happily housed in convincingly authentic pack ice. Special events and temporary exhibitions take place and there are various multimedia presentations.

The aim of Océanoplis is to educate as well as amuse. Some visitors detect, with regret, a recent trend towards mere entertainment. For all that, it's a worthwhile place to go to, and is easily the best of its kind in Brittany despite much competition and rather steep entrance charges.

➕ 3C ✉ Port de Plaisance du Moulin-Blanc, 2km (1.2 miles) east of city centre ☎ 02 98 34 40 40 🕐 Jul, Aug daily 9–7; times vary rest of year. Last tickets sold one hour before closing time ✋ Expensive 🍴 Several on-site eating places: restaurant, self-service cafe, terrace, takeaway (€–€€) – no entrance charge 🚌 3, 15 from city centre ℹ Place de la Liberté, 02 98 44 24 96

8 Presqu'île de Crozon

www.crozon.com

Interesting museums and small, low-key resorts with good fish restaurants add to the natural attractions of one of Finistère's most exhilarating coastal headlands.

This hammerhead peninsula lunges towards the Atlantic in a lather of wave-lashed fury, the foaming tongue of Finistère's mad-dog profile. It forms part of the Parc Naturel Régional d'Armorique, and has some spectacular scenery.

The old town of Le Faou makes a good starting point. Detour though the wooded estuary scenery around Térénez to the romantically set ruins of the **Abbaye de Landévennec** at the mouth of the Aulne. There's a small museum on monastic history and a Benedictine community occupies modern premises near by.

The cider museum and parish close at Argol, and the **Musée de l'École Rurale** at Trégarvan (a typical village schoolroom of the early 20th century), are worth a visit too.

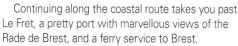

Continuing along the coastal route takes you past Le Fret, a pretty port with marvellous views of the Rade de Brest, and a ferry service to Brest.

Crozon is of no great interest, but the jagged headlands beyond (Pointe des Espagnols, Pointe de Pen-Hir and Pointe de Dinan) vie with each other for coastal charisma. The road to Pen-Hir passes the Alignements de Lagatjar (a group of standing stones). Camaret-sur-Mer is a little lobster port sheltered by a natural shingle bank called the Sillon. Here is a miniature Vauban fortress (a UNESCO World Heritage Site since 2008) with a small exhibition, and a clutch of good fish restaurants.

Morgat, a tuna-fishing port turned yachting haven, is another attractive resort with a sandy beach. Boat excursions from here visit caves with vivid mineral colourations. More gorgeous sandy beaches can be found along the southern coast.

➕ 3D 🍴 Le Mutin Gourmand (€€–€€€), place de l'Église, 02 98 27 06 51 🚌 Brest–Camaret or Quimper–Camaret via Crozon 🚢 Boat trips/ferry services from Le Fret, Camaret and Morgat

ℹ Boulevard de Pralognan, Crozon, 02 98 27 07 92; Camaret, 02 98 27 93 60; and seasonal office at Morgat, 02 98 27 29 49

Musée de l'Ancienne Abbaye de Landévennec
✉ Abbaye de Landévennec ☎ 02 98 27 35 90 🕐 Jul, Aug daily 10–7; Apr–Jun Sun–Fri 10–6; Oct–Mar Sun 10–5 (Sun–Fri 10–5 during school holidays) ✋ Inexpensive

Musée de l'École Rurale
✉ Trégarvan ☎ 02 98 26 04 72 🕐 Mid-Feb to Jun Sun–Fri 2–6; Oct, Nov 2–5; Dec to mid-Feb Mon–Fri 2–5 ✋ Inexpensive

9 Quimper

www.quimper-tourisme.com

Cornouaille's capital is one of Brittany's most charming historic cities, a pleasure for shopping and strolling.

Good road and rail links, even an international airport, make Quimper easily accessible by public transport. A day trip gives ample time to enjoy its quintessentially Breton atmosphere, especially on market day. It's a lively place with plenty of cultural activity, most noticeable during its weeklong summer Festival de Cornouaille, when Breton costume is *de rigueur*, and Celtic folk groups converge from far and wide.

The Breton name for the town derives from the word *kemper*, meeting place of rivers. The Steir and Odet run throughout the old quarter lined with pavement cafes and brasseries. Quimper is a good place for gourmet food shopping and dining. On the south bank of the Odet (where you'll find the tourist office) rises Mount Frugy, a wooded hill with panoramic picnic potential.

Crossing the river into the old town, the twin-spired Cathédrale St-Corentin (under restoration) makes an immediate impact. Near by, the **Musée Départemental Breton** displays an

extensive collection of pottery, costumes and furniture. The **Musée des Beaux-Arts,** in the town hall, contains an assortment of Pont-Aven School art. The old quarter stretches mainly west of the cathedral, past flower-decked houses and *hotels particuliers* (mansions).

Quimper dates from Roman times, when a settlement called *Aquilonia* grew up on the site of present-day Locmaria, where Quimper's ceramics industry developed, producing handpainted *paysan* designs of blue and yellow flowers or birds. The oldest of its factories is the Faïencerie HB-Henriot (tel: 02 98 90 09 36, www.hb-henriot.com, tours Mar–Oct). The Musée de la Faïence (tel: 02 98 90 12 72, www.quimper-faiences.com) has a superb display of Quimper ware.

✚ 5E 🍴 Crêperie Vieux Quimper (€), 20 rue Verdelet, 02 98 95 31 34 🚌 A major bus route hub from all parts of Brittany 🚉 Principal SNCF station 🚤 Boat trips on the Odet

ℹ️ Place de la Résistance, 02 98 53 04 05

Musée Départemental Breton

✉️ 1 rue du Roi Gradlon ☎ 02 98 95 21 60 🕐 Jun–Sep daily 9–6; Oct–May 9–12, 2–5 (closed Sun am, Mon and public hols) 🎫 Inexpensive

Musée des Beaux-Arts

✉️ 40 place St-Corentin ☎ 02 98 95 45 20 🕐 Jul, Aug daily 10–7; Sep–Jun Wed–Mon 10–12, 2–6;. closed Sun am Nov–Mar 🎫 Moderate

10 St-Malo

www.saint-malo-tourisme.com
www.ville-saint-malo.fr

The most appealing of any of the Channel ports, the walled citadel of St-Malo deserves more than a cursory glance en route to the ferry terminal, and there's plenty to see near by.

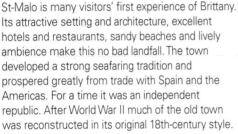

St-Malo is many visitors' first experience of Brittany. Its attractive setting and architecture, excellent hotels and restaurants, sandy beaches and lively ambience make this no bad landfall. The town developed a strong seafaring tradition and prospered greatly from trade with Spain and the Americas. For a time it was an independent republic. After World War II much of the old town was reconstructed in its original 18th-century style.

The walled city *(intra muros)* is the most interesting part. Park outside the walls and explore on foot. A rampart walk gives a splendid overview of the port's setting. On the seaward side lie sandy beaches and tidal islets. The main points of interest are the Cathédrale St-Vincent and the Château de la Duchesse Anne near the Porte St-Vincent, which contains the **Musée de la Ville** (town museum).

West of the walled town, the St-Servan district is worth a visit for marvellous views of the port and marina from the Aleth headland. The Tour Solidor contains a small museum dedicated to Cape Horn sailors. East of St-Malo are the resorts of Paramé and Rothéneuf, with good beaches. In Rothéneuf visit the Manoir Limoëlou, former home of Jacques Cartier, discoverer of Canada.

✠ 13C 🍴 La Brigantine (€€), 13 rue de Dinan,
02 99 56 82 82 🚌 Rennes, Mont-St-Michel, Dinard,
the Emerald Coast, Fougères, Dinan 🚆 Rennes,
Normandy (TVG link to Paris) ⛴ Brittany Ferries
(Portsmouth, UK); shuttle ferry to Dinard; regular services to
Channel Isles, Weymouth, Poole; Rance river trips to Dinan
✈ Dinard–St-Malo airport; Aurigny and Ryanair services to
UK/Channel Isles
ℹ Esplanade St-Vincent, 0 825 13 52 00

Musée de la Ville

☎ 02 99 40 71 57 🕐 Apr–Sep daily 10–12, 2–6; Oct–Mar
Tue–Sat 10–12, 2–6 ✋ Moderate

Best things to do

Good places to have lunch

Ar Men Du (€–€€€)

A splendid coastal location overlooking an unspoiled beach and tidal island at this stylish little restaurant-with-rooms. Fish fans should opt for the *Menu de Glénan*.

✉ Raguenez-Plage, Port-Manec'h, Névez ☎ 02 98 06 84 22; www.men-du.com 🕐 Daily 12:30–2, 7:30–9; closed Tue–Wed lunch Nov to mid-Mar

Le Bistrot du Bac (€–€€)

One thing you won't forget is the view across the wooded Odet estuary from this place. Steak followed by an *île flottante* (meringue islands with custard) goes down well. Reserve ahead.

✉ 19 rue du Bac, Ste-Marine ☎ 02 98 56 34 79; www.hoteldubac.fr 🕐 Daily 12–2, 7–9:30

Le Bistrot du Marin (€–€€)

Join a throng of sailing folk tucking into pizza and huge platters of seafood at this panoramic restaurant overlooking the marina.

✉ 34 cours des Quais, La Trinité-sur-Mer ☎ 02 97 55 73 23; www.hotel-ostrea.com 🕐 Tue–Sat 12–2:30, 7–9:30, Sun 12–2:30

Café Breton (€–€€)

This charming little bistro is always packed with satisfied locals. Friendly, genuine service and excellent cooking. Reservations advised.

✉ 14 rue Nantaise, Rennes ☎ 02 99 30 74 95 🕐 Tue–Fri 12–3, 7–11, Mon, Sat 12–3; closed Sun

Café Terrasses (€–€€)

Overlooking the scenic port, this upbeat bistro is perfect for an informal meal at any time of day. Salads, omelettes and mussels are popular dishes.

✉ 2–4 rue du Quai, Dinan ☎ 02 96 39 09 60 🕐 Daily 12–2, 7–9; closed mid-Nov to mid-Dec. Sep–Jun closed Sun eve, Mon, Tue eve

La Cigale (€–€€€)

Classic brasserie with superb *fin-de-siècle* decor. Perfect for smart seafood lunches, cakes or after-theatre suppers.

✉ 4 place Graslin, Nantes ☎ 02 51 84 94 94; www.lacigale.com ⏰ Daily 7:30am–12:30am. Lunch served from 11:45am

Continental (€–€€)

One of the best of the seafood restaurants in this famous oyster port, with views over the oyster beds.

✉ 4 quai Thomas, Cancale ☎ 02 99 89 60 16; www.hotel-cancale.com ⏰ Daily 11:45–2, 7–9:30. Closed Wed, Thu Oct–Apr

Le Décollé (€–€€)

Enjoy a wonderful view at this dramatic bit of Emerald Coast. Try the sole with seaweed butter or artichokes with bacon and cider.

✉ Pointe du Décollé, St-Lunaire ☎ 02 99 46 01 70, www.restaurantdudecolle.com ⏰ Daily 12:15–2, 7:15–9, closed Mon, Tue Sep–Apr

Mare aux Oiseaux (€–€€€)

This smart, thatched, hotel-restaurant in the Grande Brière serves an inventive range of regional dishes using local ingredients. Try eels in salted butter.

✉ 162 Île de Fedrun, St-Joachim ☎ 02 40 88 53 01; www.mareauxoiseaux.fr ⏰ Daily 2:30–2, 7:30–9:30; closed Mon lunch

Le Vivier (€–€€)

Aside from the fresh-out-of-the-water crabs, mussels and oysters, the main reason to come to this cliff-perched restaurant is for the view over Belle-Île and the 'wild coast'. Children's menus also available.

✉ Côte Sauvage, Quiberon ☎ 02 97 50 12 60 ⏰ Apr–Sep daily 12-–3, 7–9; closed Dec–Jan; eves in Oct, Nov and Feb, Mar (except Sat, Sun)

Top activities

Canal- and river-boating: More than 600km (370 miles) of navigable waterways provide an exceptional network of routes, and boats can be rented in many places. Two important waterway junctions are Redon and Dinan. For details of boat hire contact Bateaux Sans-Permis (tel: 04 67 13 19 62, www.bateaux-sans-permis.com).

Canoeing and kayaking: Sea, lake and river canoeing is possible in Brittany. Varec'h, in the Gulf of Morbihan, offers hire and tuition (tel: 02 97 57 16 16, www.bretagne-kayak.com).

Cycling: Brittany's gentler gradients will appeal to non-masochists, but there's mountain-biking too for intrepid off-roaders. For organized cycling holidays contact Breton Bikes (tel: 02 96 24 86 72, www.bretonbikes.com).

Fishing: Besides being one of Brittany's most important industries, sea fishing is a recreational activity, ranging in nature from low-tide *pêche-à-pied* with bucket and rake for shellfish to high-tech sport-fishing off the coast. Brittany's many inland waterways provide lots of

opportunities for freshwater angling. For fishing holidays and trips in Finistére visit www.fishandfunbrittany.com.

Golf: Brittany's golf courses range from the exclusive historic links at Dinard to the challengingly designed modern Baden course in Morbihan. Visit www.brittanytourism.com for details.

Horse-riding: The varied terrain offers a magnificent choice of trekking possibilities. For beach trekking on the Côtes d'Armor contact Univers Ponies (tel: 02 96 20 37 76, www.univers-ponies.com).

Sailing: Brittany's long and varied littoral with its challenging hazards of reefs and currents make it a focus for keen sailors. The coast is studded with well-equipped marinas. The sheltered southern waters around Bénodet, Îles de Glénan and Quiberon are ideal places to learn. For sailing holidays and courses in Camaret-sur-Mer contact Brittany Sailing (tel: 02 98 17 01 31, www.brittanysail.co.uk).

Thalassotherapy: Want to lose weight, give up smoking or simply de-stress? Some seawater-based spa treatments are just what the doctor ordered. The flagship centre is Miramar Crouesty (tel: 02 97 53 49 00, www.miramarcrouesty.com).

Walking: Nearly 5,000km (3,110 miles) of footpaths make walking Brittany's most popular recreational activity. Coastal walks, canal towpaths and forest trails cater for all fitness levels For routes and guidebooks contact Brittany Walks (tel: 02 98 24 15 19, www.brittanywalks.com).

Watersports: Surfing, windsurfing and scuba-diving are available in many coastal resorts. Most cater for beginners and experts. Visit www.ecole-surf-bretagne.fr for surf schools around Brittany.

a drive along the Armorique Corniche

This route spans the coastal borderlands of Finistère and Côtes d'Armor, through a landscape of sandy beaches, rocky headlands, fishing ports and estuary scenery.

Take the D786 southwest of Lannion to St-Michel-en-Grève (11km/7 miles), then detour briefly inland on the D30 to Ploumilliau (4km/2.5 miles).

Ploumilliau's 17th-century church contains an unnerving sculpture of Ankou (the Breton representation of Death), ready with scythe and spade to gather in his human crop.

Retrace your route to the D786, and continue westwards along the Lieu de Grève.

St-Michel-en-Grève's beach is a magnificent 4km (2.5-mile) crescent of firm, perfectly golden sand stretching 2km (1.2 miles) out to sea at low tide. Sand-yachting is a popular local sport. At the west end of the bay, St-Efflam's chapel has a domed fountain dedicated to the local hermit saint.

Leave the main D786 at St-Efflam and follow the corniche route to Locquirec (D42).

This attractive resort and fishing port occupies a scenic headland where affluent villas take advantage of the views. Just west of the village, more glorious beaches are visible from roadside viewpoints at Marc'h Sammet (good picnic spots on a clear day).

Continue on minor roads, hugging the coast as closely as possible, to St-Jean-du-Doigt.

St Jean-du-Doigt's parish close has a triumphal arch and a beautiful Renaissance fountain depicting St John baptizing Christ. John the Baptist's index finger was allegedly brought here in the 15th century and is kept in the church.

Take the D46 northwards to Plougasnou, then trickle round more coastal lanes to the Cairn de Barnenez.

Beyond more pretty fishing ports (Le Diben, Térénez) lies the impressive Cairn de Barnenez. This megalithic site of terraced granite has 11 separate burial chambers overlooking the Baie de Morlaix (there are excellent guided tours).

Continue down the D76 to Morlaix.

Distance 70km (43 miles)
Time Allow half a day, with time for a walk or picnic, and a visit to the Cairn de Barnenez
Start point Lannion ✚ 8B
End point Morlaix ✚ 6B
Lunch Grand Hôtel des Bains (€–€€€), Locquirec, 02 98 67 41 02

Top souvenir ideas

Antiques: Bric-a-brac shops and markets abound in Brittany, and while furniture may be difficult to transport, there are plenty of smaller keepsakes to buy, from wooden spoons to butter-moulds.

Cakes, *crêpes* and biscuits: Classic recipes like *kouig namann* or *far breton* are on sale in all bakeries. Even the famous Breton pancakes *(crêpes* or *galettes)* are packaged ready to take home. Pont-Aven is a leading centre of biscuit manufacture – its buttery cookies are sold in beautifully decorated tins, themselves a collectable item.

Celtic music: If you attend any local festivals, you'll probably hear some typical Breton folk music played on mysterious instruments like the *bombarde* and the *biniou*. There's been a great revival of interest in Celtic music, and many shops sell music recordings.

Cider, beer and wine: Brittany's main tipple is cider, produced from the lush orchards of the Rance and Odet valleys. Enthusiastic micro-breweries like Coreff and Dremmwell sell interesting

real ales. Other drinks include *chouchen*, a strongly alcoholic mead, and *lambig* a powerful cider brandy, while Nantes is the land of the crisp white wines of Muscadet.

Faïencerie: The most famous Breton pottery comes from Quimper, and is hand-decorated with *paysanne* designs of flowers, birds and costumed figures. Local firms like HB-Henriot (➤ 53) offer guided tours and discounted stock in their showrooms.

Household linen: Brittany has a long tradition of textile manufacture. The hempen rigging of many a galleon once hailed from Locronan, but these days you're more likely to find napkins and tablecloths in its tourist shops. Pont-l'Abbé in Finistère specializes in hand-embroidered linen and lace.

Knitwear: Classic marine stripes in red and navy characterize many Breton sweaters and separates. High-quality brands like Saint James and Armor-Lux are widely available.

Seafood: If lugging home a sack of live oysters or mussels seems impractical, don't despair. Firms like La Belle-Iloise produce a superb range of gourmet fish products, smoked, cured, marinaded and enticingly packed in tins and jars.

Seaweed products: It's amazing what you can do with seaweed. Brest's Océanopolis (➤ 48–49) explains some of its many culinary, cosmetic and pharmaceutical uses, and in places like Roscoff, shops sell locally made soaps, lotions and foodstuffs based on some of Brittany's hundreds of species.

Weatherproof clothing: Fishermen's oilskins and yachtsman's jackets besides being strong, warm and comfortable, are very fashionable too. Look for names like Guy Cotten in harbourfront Comptoir de la Mer shops.

Best beaches

La Baule: The tourist authorities claim the resort's beach is the most beautiful in Europe. Stretching for 7km (4 miles), it shelves so gently that you can walk 100m (110yds) into the sea within your depth.

Brignogan-Plages: The eight linked beaches of this quiet resort make a perfect place to unwind. Strewn with weirdly shaped boulders, this coastline is full of sheltered natural coves and rockpools.

Carantec: This smart but relaxing family resort enjoys a lovely stretch of coastal scenery on the west side of Morlaix Bay, and a choice of six different beaches. There's lots for children in summer, and plenty of boat trips and sports. Explore the creeks of Île Callot at low tide, or take a sea canoe around the sheltered waters.

Carnac-Plage: While many visitors head for the megaliths, this sheltered beach resort backed by pine trees is ideal for families. With watersports, children's shows, evening markets and a thalassotherapy centre, there's plenty to entertain.

Cherreuix: The firm, flat expanses that fringe the Baie de Mont-St-Michel are a great place to watch sand-yachting. Make sure you don't get in the way – these craft can reach incredible speeds in a high wind.

Dinard: The best beaches here are perhaps the Plage de l'Écluse, immortalized by Picasso and decked with chic stripy beach tents in summer, and the dazzling Plage du Prieuré at the rocky mouth of the River Rance.

Plage de la Torche: This vast and lonely beach on the wild Penmarc'h coast is a renowned windsurfing venue, but it's definitely not for novices. Nothing stops the Atlantic breakers here, and in a gale it's unforgettable.

Ploumanac'h: The tiny beach of St-Guirec is scarcely big enough for all its summer visitors, but the views of this extraordinary bit of Pink Granite coastline are absolute magic. Enjoy them from the Coste Mor restaurant or the coastguard's watchpath round the rocks.

Ste-Anne-la-Palud: This tranquil seascape, unspoiled by development, is best enjoyed towards sunset when you can have it to yourself beside the little chapel of St Anne.

Le Val-André: Freshly polished by the retreating tide, Le Val-André's fine pale sands gleam mirror-bright against the setting sun. Perfect for either beachcombers or watersports enthusiasts.

Places to take the children

Armoripark

As well as several outdoor pools and waterslides, this leisure complex near Guingamp also has trampolines, pedal karts, mini-golf, a toddlers' playground and a pets' corner.

✉ Bégard ☎ 02 96 45 36 36; www.armoripark.com 🕐 Jul, Aug daily 11–7; times vary rest of year; closed Oct–Mar

Cité de la Voile

This fascinating, interactive sailing museum opened in 2008. Learn how to navigate or design a boat, then take a trip in a sailboat with a qualified skipper. Information in English.

✉ Keroman submarine base, Lorient ☎ 02 97 65 56 56; www.citevoile-tabarly.com 🕐 Jul, Aug daily 10-8; Sep–Jun Tue–Sun 10–6; closed Jan

Domaine de Ménez-Meur

A conservation park with a varied collection of fauna, from wolves and wild boar to Ouessant's dwarf black sheep. Adventure playground, nature trails, pony rides and more.

✉ Near Hanvec in the Monts d'Arrée, off the D18 ☎ 02 98 68 81 71 🕐 Jul, Aug daily 10–7; May, Jun, Sep 10–6; times vary rest of year; closed Dec–Feb

Haliotika

Learn about the world of sea fishing in one of Finistère's main fishing ports. Visit a fish auction followed by a langoustine tasting. Tours in English in summer.

✉ Le Port, Le Guilvinec ☎ 02 98 58 28 38; www.haliotika.com 🕐 Apr–Oct times vary; closed Nov–Mar.

Les Machines de l'Île

Enjoy a walk around the Île de Nantes in a 50-tonne mechanical elephant 12m (40ft) high, before visiting the gallery to meet sea monsters and other fantastical animalchines.

✉ Boulevard Léon Bureau, Île de Nantes ☎ 0810 12 12 25; www.lesmachines-nantes.fr 🕐 Check online; closed Mon and Jan to mid-Feb

Musée de Bretagne/Espace des Sciences

A museum complex with engaging exhibits on the region's history. Toys, games and comic strips. Planetarium and discovery zone.

✉ 10 cours des Alliés, Rennes ☎ 02 23 40 66 70, www.musee-bretagne.fr; 02 23 40 66 40, www.espace-sciences.org ⏰ Tue–Sun, times vay

Parc de Branféré

Some 1,500 animals wander freely through the attractively landscaped park of a château. Lots of children's activities.

✉ Le Guerno (25km/15.5 miles southwest of Vannes) ☎ 02 97 42 94 66; www.branfere.com ⏰ Feb to mid-Nov daily, times vary

Parc des Grands Chênes/Port Miniature

This forest leisure complex has an aerial adventure playground and a boating lake. Waymarked trails, pony-rides.

✉ Base de Loisirs Forêt de Villecartier (15km/9 miles southeast of Dol-de-Bretagne) ☎ 06 88 72 73 40 (park), www.parcdesgrandschens.fr; 02 99 98 37 24 (port) ⏰ Check websites for opening times

Parc de Préhistoire de Bretagne

Take a trip back in time and encounter dinosaurs, the first inhabitants of Brittany and discover how the region's ancient standing stones were transported.

✉ Malansac ☎ 02 97 43 34 17; www.prehistoire.com ⏰ Apr–Sep daily 10:30–7; Oct Sun 1–6:30; closed Nov–Mar

Le Village Gaulois

Over 20 Gallic-themed activities in a reconstructed village with thatched huts and wooden boats.

✉ Pleumeur-Bodou (10km/6 miles from Lannion) ☎ 02 96 91 83 95 ⏰ Jul, Aug daily 10:30–7; Apr–Jun, Sep Sun–Fri 2–6; closed Oct–Easter

Best parish closes

Brasparts: (➤ 93) has a fine calvary depicting St Michael slaying a dragon.

Guéhenno: This charmingly naïve calvary was damaged in the Revolution, and restored by the local priest. The cock symbolizes Peter's denial of Christ.

Guimiliau: (➤ 46–47) One of Brittany's most striking parish closes – a tour de force of Renaissance sculpture.

La Martyre: An ancient parish close with an interesting ossuary and triumphal door. Extensive interior decoration.

Pencran: A 16th-century ossuary, carved porch and balconied belfry distinguish this church. The calvary is incorporated into the surrounding wall.

Pleyben: Very large calvary with various scenes depicting the life of Jesus from the Nativity to the Passion, and handsome church interior (carved beams and altarpieces).

Plougastel-Daoulas: A large, elaborate calvary and plague cross. Carvings of Catell Gollet (➤ 47).

La Roche-Maurice: A classical ossuary with an Ankou figure of death, and twin-galleried belfry. Lovely Renaissance rood screen in the church.

St-Thégonnec: A fine calvary and triumphal arch, and splendid church interior too. Notice the local saint with his tame wolf.

Sizun: This church has a triumphal arch and a 16th-century ossuary, with rich panelling inside the church (➤ 92).

Best pardons and festivals

PARDONS

A *pardon* is a religious festival that celebrates a saint or a church. Pilgrims are pardoned for their sins, hence the name.

Camaret-sur-Mer: *1st Sun in Sep* This little lobster-fishing resort on the Crozon peninsula combines its fervent Pardon de Notre-Dame-de-Rocamadour with a Blessing of the Sea ceremony. The focus is a picturesque seaside chapel where sailor pilgrims made landfall in the 11th century (www.camaret-sur-mer.com).

Le Folgoët: *1st or 2nd Sun in Sep* The Grand Pardon here is a huge and splendid affair with lots of Breton coiffes, costumes and banners. Pilgrims gather for Mass with Breton hymns on the village green. It commemorates the legend of Salaün, a local simpleton who could speak only the words Ave Maria. When he died a white lily sprang from his grave bearing the Latin inscription, indicating his sainthood (http://notre-dame-folgoet.cef.fr).

Locronan: *2nd Sun in Jul* Every year locals celebrate their patron St Ronan by re-enacting his daily penitential climb up the hill near the town. This pilgrimage is called the Petite Troménie. Every sixth year (last in 2007) there's a longer and more elaborate Grande Troménie around the hill, stopping at 12 Stations of the Cross (www.locronan.org).

Ste-Anne-la-Palud: *Last weekend in Aug* The Grand Pardon here celebrates the mother of the Virgin, Brittany's patroness. Pilgrims convene at a chapel by the beach to pay homage in traditional Breton costume (www.tourisme-porzay.com).

Tréguier: *3rd Sun in May* St Yves, patron saint of lawyers, championed the poor. This *pardon* commemorates the anniversary of his death. A reliquary is wheeled out of the church and carried through the streets to his birthplace (www.ville-treguier.fr).

FESTIVALS

Festival des Filets Bleus: Concarneau *3rd week in Aug*
Commemorates the harsh times in the early 20th century when
the sardine shoals vanished and the local fishing industry
collapsed. It is now a lively folk festival (http://filetsbleus.free.fr).

Festival InterCeltique: Lorient *Early to mid-Aug* This gathering of
all things Celtic attracts visitors for a feast of traditional music,
dancing, and folklore (www.festival-interceltique.com).

Fête de Cornouaille: Quimper *Mid- to late Jul* One of Brittany's
most important cultural events, lasting about nine days. Thousands
of artists arrive from all over Europe to put on concerts, exhibitions
and entertainments (www.festival-cornouaille.com).

Fête des Remparts: Dinan *Late Jul* This biennial festival (held in
even-numbered years) turns the fortifications of the old walled
town into a blaze of colourful medieval pageantry, with jousting,
banquets, fairs and fireworks (www.fete-remparts-dinan.com).

Les Tombées de la Nuit: Rennes *Early Jul* Breton culture is
celebrated in a huge 10-day art-rock festival involving music, dance
and theatre (www.lestombeesdelanuit.com).

Exploring

For the Celtic tribes who first settled here during the Iron Age, Brittany was *Armor* – the Land by the Sea. Generations of Bretons have earned a living from seafaring and today the waves cast up new sources of revenue in the ferry terminals of Roscoff and St-Malo as thousands of British and Irish visitors come to Brittany.

The Emerald Coast around St-Malo, the russet rocks of the Pink Granite Coast further west, and the lush, wooded estuaries of Cornouaille are some of the most charismatic stretches. Finistère's deadly reefs lie half-submerged, waiting for Atlantic storms, treacherous currents or bewildering sea fogs to serve up their prey. The main feature of Morbihan's coastline is the huge tidal lagoon called the Golfe du Morbihan, scattered with hundreds of islets. Loire-Atlantique's low-lying shores boast the biggest, and some claim, Europe's most beautiful beach at La Baule.

Finistère

**Finistère is the most
Breton part of Brittany, a land
of priests and pagans,
pierced steeples and
spectacular parish closes, where
fervent piety mingles with ancient
superstition. Here, more than
anywhere, you may find traditional
customs and costumes, and hear Breton spoken. The
fertile *Ceinture d'Orée* (Golden Belt) stretches along the
north coast, producing early vegetables, but Brittany's
age-old maritime economy still figures large in the
fishing ports of Douarnenez, Concarneau and Roscoff.**

The dramatic extremities of Crozon and Sizun make memorable
touring, and the islands of Ouessant and Batz have their own
quiet charm. Inland, the wild uplands of the Monts d'Arrée and
Montagnes Noires are a chance to escape coastal crowds; a few
remnants of Brittany's ancient forests survive at Huelgoat. In the
south, the lush wooded estuaries of the rivers Odet and the Aven
create the idyllic watercolours immortalized by Pont-Aven's
19th-century artists.

BÉNODET

In the Middle Ages, Bénodet's income sprang from trading salt, fish and wine. Today its economic mainstay is tourism. Apart from its lighthouses and a scrap of fortress, the town has few notable sights or historic buildings. Its popularity is based on the attractions of its natural setting at the mouth of the wooded Odet estuary, and a series of excellent beaches. Families converge to take advantage of Bénodet's resort amenities in summer, which include sailing in Le Letty's tidal lagoon. The **Musée du Bord de Mer** explains the history of yachting and sailing at Bénodet. For more seclusion, take the graceful modern bridge or shuttle ferry across the river to Ste-Marine. Boat trips up the River Odet, or to the Îles de Glénan in the Baie de Concarneau, are highly recommended.

www.benodet.fr

✚ 4F 🍴 Les Bains de Mer (€–€€), 11 rue Kerguelen, 02 98 57 03 41
🚌 No 16 (Quimper) 🚢 Trips on the Odet and to Îles de Glénan
ℹ 29 avenue de la Mer, 02 98 57 00 14

Musée du Bord de Mer

✉ 29 avenue de la Mer ☎ 02 98 57 00 14 🕐 Jul, Aug daily 10–1, 2–6; Sep–Jun Thu–Mon 🖐 Inexpensive

BREST

Brest's strategic location on a magnificent natural harbour (Rade de Brest) at the edge of western Europe has been its fortune, and its undoing. The Romans first spotted its potential and built a camp in the 3rd century. The settlement was fortified by the counts of Léon in the 12th century, and occupied by the English for part of the Hundred Years War. Louis XIII chose it as his principal naval base in the 17th century. Brest expanded during the seafaring centuries that followed, though its harbour was maintained for defensive rather than trade purposes, and it never accrued the wealth of other Breton seaports.

During German Occupation, Brest became a U-Boat base, plaguing transatlantic convoys and becoming the unwilling target of sustained Allied bombardment towards the end of the war. When Brest fell in 1944, it was utterly devastated. Vast post-war investment has rebuilt, if not entirely revitalized the town in a functional modern style of concrete high-rises. It retains none of its former charm, but is worth a visit for its streamlined docks and roadstead views, and several interesting sights. A university town, it has plenty of cultural activities and events. Harbour cruises are highly recommended.

The castle and the neighbouring Cours Dajot promenade give excellent views of the Rade de Brest. Built between the 12th and 17th centuries, it miraculously withstood the bombs of World War II and now houses both the naval headquarters and the

Musée de la Marine (Maritime Museum). Near the castle stands the massive Pont de Recouvrance swing bridge and the 15th-century Tour Tanguy, containing a museum of Old Brest, which gives an enlightening view of how the port once looked. In the city centre, the **Musée des Beaux-Arts** (Fine Arts Museum) contains a collection of Pont-Aven paintings. On the north side of town, at Port de Plaisance du Moulin-Blanc, the **Conservatoire Botanique National** preserves endangered species. But the futuristic aquarium, Océanopolis, is the city's main attraction (➤ 48–49). **www.**brest-metropole-tourisme.fr

✚ 3C 🍴 Le Ruffe (€–€€€), 1 bis rue Yves Collet, 02 98 46 07 70
🚌 Major route-hub for public transport; many inner-city buses
⛴ Ferry to Le Fret; harbour cruises; trips to Ouessant and Camaret
🛈 Place de la Liberté, 02 98 44 24 96

Musée de la Marine

✚ *Brest 1f* ✉ Château de Brest ☎ 02 98 22 12 39;
www.musee-marine.fr ⏲ Apr–Sep daily 10–6:30; Oct–Mar
1:30–6:30; closed Jan 🖐 Moderate

Musée des Beaux-Arts

✚ *Brest 2e* ✉ 24 rue Traverse ☎ 02 98 00 87 96 ⏲ Daily
10–12, 2–6; closed Tue, Sun am and public hols 🖐 Moderate

Conservatoire Botanique National

✉ 52 allée du Bot ☎ 02 98 02 46 00; www.cbnbrest.fr
⏲ Garden daily 9–6 (until 8 in summer); greenhouses Apr–Sep
Wed, Sun 2–5:30; visitor centre 2 Jul–15 Sep Sun–Fri 2–5:30;
Apr–Jun, mid-Sep to Oct Wed, Sun 2–5:30 🖐 Free to garden and
visitor centre; inexpensive to greenhouses

CAP SIZUN

Sizun's jagged finger stretches far into the Atlantic,
ending at the Pointe du Raz, where a statue of Notre-
Dame-des-Naufragés (Our Lady of the Shipwrecked) is

aptly placed. Out to sea, the Île de Sein barely rises above the waterline, a treacherous obstacle to shipping. If you want to walk around the headland note that the rocks can be very slippery, and take binoculars if you are keen on birdwatching. The **Réserve de Goulien** is a popular destination during the nesting season, and Audierne has another large nature reserve, the **Maison de la Baie**, which organizes nature walks.

Apart from the fishing ports of Douarnenez and Audierne, there are no large settlements. Inland is quiet farmland. Audierne has a fine setting on the Goyen estuary, large fish farms (visitors welcome), and the impressive **L'Aquashow** (Breton marine species and bird shows).

www.audierne-tourisme.com

2E

Réserve de Goulien

Cap Sizun 02 98 70 13 53 Apr–Aug 10–6. Guided tours Jul–Aug daily 2:30; Apr–Jun varies Moderate

Maison de la Baie

St-Vio, Tréguennec 02 98 87 65 07 Call for times and events Moderate

L'Aquashow

Rue du Goyen, Audierne 02 98 70 03 03; www.aquarium.fr Apr–Sep daily 10–7; Oct 2–6; open school hols in winter Expensive

a drive around Cap Sizun

A drive round some of Finistère's most exciting headlands.

*From Douarnenez, take the north coast road (D7),
ducking northwards at Pointe du Millier.*

A few minutes' walk to the point offers a splendid view of
the bay. Further west, Pointe de Beuzec (accessible by car)
has similar views.

*Return to the D7 and head westwards to the Réserve
de Goulien at Cap Sizun.*

This famous bird sanctuary on a wild granite cape is best
visited between April and mid-July when a host of seabirds
rear their young on the dark rocky cliffs of Castel-ar-Roc'h.

*Return to the D7 again and continue 6km (4 miles)
westwards to the Pointe de Brézellec (north off
the road).*

Park near the lighthouse and enjoy a magnificent vantage point of serrated rocks and cliffs.

Continue west to the Pointe du Van.

A lengthy walk leads to a desolate, treeless headland of stone and moss, less spectacular than Pointe du Raz, but less crowded. The cliffs here are dangerous. One lonely hotel guards the headland.

Follow the coast road south past the Baie des Trépassés.

This sweeping crescent of firm sand may look inviting, but the currents are strong. In a gale, it's a terrifying sight.

Join the D784 and head west for 2.5km (1.5 miles) to the Pointe du Raz, the highlight of the journey.

Technically this is not quite France's most westerly point. The point snakes out to sea, ending in razor pinnacles. A path leads round the rocky point with safety ropes, but take care; the rocks are slippery and freak waves may sweep you off.

Return to Douarnenez along the D784 via Audierne, then the D765 via Pont-Croix.

Distance 80km (50 miles) – some walking
Time Allow about half a day – longer with extensive walks or picnics
Start/end point Douarnenez ✚ 4E
Lunch Hotel de la Baie des Trépassés, Pointe du Raz (€–€€), 02 98 70 61 34

CHÂTEAU DE KERJEAN

The Château de Kerjean is one of Brittany's finest Renaissance manors. Set in 20ha (50 acres) of sweeping parkland, the château's gabled roofline rises above high ramparts, beyond a drawbridge and a deep moat. It dates from the late 16th century, and suffered much damage during the Revolution, when its last *aristo* was guillotined. In 1911, it passed into State hands. Since then it has been restored and converted into a cultural centre and museum of traditional Breton furniture. As well as a film show, learn about château life in the 18th century through workshops.

http://kerjean.eklablog.com

✚ 5B ✉ St-Vougay ☎ 02 98 69 93 69 ⏲ Jul, Aug daily 10–7; off season times vary ✋ Moderate

CONCARNEAU

Fishing is on the decline in Concarneau (once one of France's most important ports), but it still has a sizeable fleet and lands varied catches in the modern, shed-like fish market by the Arrière-Port. If you arrive early enough, you can see the *criée* (fish auction) in full swing. An organization called **À l'Assaut des Remparts** offers guided tours (some in English) of the old town, including visits to the harbour, a working trawler and the quayside fish auction. The evening tours are particularly interesting, when you can see the boats arrive to unload their catches after midnight.

Concarneau's most charming district is the medieval old town, or Ville Close, on a rocky island protected by granite ramparts and a fortified bridge. Tourists crowd over the drawbridge to explore quaint old streets and attractive souvenir shops. The Ville Close's best sight is the **Musée de la Pêche,** a well-displayed exhibition on the fishing industry with ancient sardine tins and giant scooping nets. An old trawler reveals the spartan conditions of life at sea.

Beaches stretch either side of the town – head for Les Sables Blancs. Boat trips from Concarneau visit the Îles de Glénan and the Odet estuary. In late August, Concarneau's Fête des Filets Bleus (Blue Nets Festival, ➤ 73) attracts many visitors.

www.tourismeconcarneau.fr

✚ 5F 🍴 Chez Armande (€–€€€), 15 bis avenue Dr Nicolas, 02 98 97 00 76
🚌 No 14 (Quimper–Pont-Aven); No 20 (Rosporden) ⛴ Odet, Îles de Glénan and bay cruises
🛈 Quai d'Aiguillon, 02 98 97 01 44

A l'Assaut des Remparts

✉ Quai Criée ☎ 02 98 50 55 18; www.alassautdesremparts.fr 💰 Moderate
❓ Escorted tours

Musée de la Pêche

✉ 3 rue Vauban, Ville-Close ☎ 02 98 97 10 20 🕐 Jul, Aug daily 9:30–8; Apr–Jun, Sep 10–6; Feb, Mar, Oct, Nov 10–12, 2–6 💰 Moderate

GUIMILIAU

Best places to see, pages 46–47.

ÎLE D'OUESSANT

Ouessant is the largest of the islands scattered off the coast of Finistère (Batz, Moléne, Sein and the Glénan archipelago), a treacherous obstacle course for one of the world's busiest shipping lanes. Despite all the lighthouses and warning beacons that guard the reefs, disasters still occur, notably the *Amoco Cadiz*, which foundered in 1978, and the *Erika* in 1999.

Ouessant (anglicized as Ushant) is one of Finistère's remotest communities, yet it is easily reached on a fast ferry from Le Conquet or Brest. In fine weather (preferably calm!) a day trip is highly recommendable. Ouessant's traditional matriarchal way of life has all but vanished on the mainland, and although the island now relies increasingly on tourism for its revenue, the older social patterns still persist. It is also an important marine conservation area, and forms part of the Parc Naturel Régional d'Armorique. Ouessant's maritime climate is surprisingly mild in winter. Seaweed processing is a local industry.

Ferry passengers alight at the Baie du Stiff, where two lighthouses (ancient and modern) guard the eastern headlands. From here the best way to explore the island is by bike (for hire at the port or the main village of Lampaul). Ouessant (7km by 4km/4 miles by 2.5 miles) is rather too large to see on foot in a single day and simple accommodation and restaurants can be found in Lampaul. The churchyard here contains a monument to the many islanders lost at sea.

The main sights on the island are the **Ecomusée du Niou,** housed in two tiny cottages displaying a typical seafaring home of the 19th century, and numerous costumes, tools and other exhibits. On the west coast, the Phare du Créac'h contains a lighthouse museum, the **Musée des Phares et Balises,** highlighting the coastal warning system of western Brittany.

The remaining pleasures of Ouessant lie mostly out of doors, in its dramatic coastal scenery, wildlife and open heathland where its small, black sheep roam freely. Many of the white cottages have blue doors and shutters, the colour of the protecting Virgin's robes.

www.ot-ouessant.fr

⊞ 1B ▮▮ Ty Korn (€–€€), Lampaul

ℹ Place de l'Église, Lampaul, 02 98 48 87 33

Ecomusée du Niou

✉ Niou Uhella ☎ 02 98 48 86 37 🕔 Jun–Aug daily 11–6; Apr, May, Sep 11–5; Oct–Mar Tue–Sun 1:30–5.30 (except school hols daily 11–5)

🖐 Inexpensive (joint ticket with Musée des Phares et Balises available)

Musée des Phares et Balises

✉ Phare du Créac'h ☎ 02 98 48 80 70 🕔 Times as Ecomusée du Niou

🖐 Inexpensive (joint ticket with Ecomusée du Niou available)

LOCRONAN

Even when besieged by summer visitors, Locronan's charms are undeniable. Its Renaissance square of gold-grey buildings is as pretty as a filmset, which, indeed, it has been from time to time. Many of the former merchants' houses have been converted into shops, restaurants and hotels. A browse through its craft studios is an ideal way of choosing Breton souvenirs.

Locronan's wealth came from the manufacture of sailcloth, and for a period in the 17th century it single-handedly supplied much of Europe's maritime rigging. When Louis XIV abolished its monopoly, Locronan's economy collapsed. The church of St-Ronan is one of the most striking monuments, in 15th-century Ogival Flamboyant style. Stained glass marks scenes of the Passion, while the carved pulpit recounts its patron saint's life. St Ronan was an Irish missionary, and his penitential climb each day up the hill behind the town is re-enacted by annual processions called *Troménies*.

A short distance from Locronan, the seaside chapel of Ste-Anne-la-Palud is the scene of one of the finest *pardon* ceremonies in Brittany (➤ 72), with torchlit processions and Breton costumes. The object of veneration is a painted granite statue of St Anne dating from 1548.

www.locronan.org

✚ 4E 🍴 Plenty of choice in and around the church square, such as Ty Coz (€), place de l'Eglise 🚌 No 10 (Quimper–Plomodiern–Camaret)
ℹ Place de la Mairie, 02 98 91 70 14

MONTS D'ARRÉE

These ancient granite hills were once as high as the Alps: now the elements have eroded them to rounded stumps covered with gorse moors. The less accessible stretches provide wildlife sanctuaries, and you may encounter deer, otters and wild boar.

Much of the Monts d'Arrée massif forms part of the Parc Naturel Régional d'Armorique, encompassing hills and woodland, the Aulne estuary, the coast of Crozon and the Ouessant archipelago. A dozen or so little museums sprinkled throughout the park show various aspects of traditional rural life. The park's main information centre is at Ménez-Meur, a wooded estate with a zoo park, and which holds temporary exhibitions on Breton life. Huelgoat is the main community of a last vestige of Brittany's *argoat* or inland forest. Devastated by the hurricane of 1987, there are few venerable trees left, but giant mossy boulders, fern-filled grottoes and a placid lake add interest to local walks.

www.pnr-armorique.fr

✚ 5–6C 🍴 Les Voyageurs (€–€€), 2 rue Argoat, Sizun, 02 98 68 80 35
🚌 Nos 52 and 61 serve Huelgoat, no scheduled routes cross the wilder zones
ℹ Ménez-Meur, 02 98 68 81 71

MORLAIX

The town's location at the head of a dramatic estuary gave it a leading role in the maritime trade of the Renaissance, and from embryonic origins as a Gaullish defence camp it burgeoned into a thriving port prospering on fishing, linen, shipbuilding, tobacco-smuggling – and piracy. Morlaix was a corsair town and its daring raids on foreign shipping provoked reprisals. After the English sacked the town in 1522, Morlaix adopted a truculent motto (a pun on its name): 'S'ils te mordent, mords-les' ('If they bite you, bite them back!'), and constructed the Château du Taureau to guard the bay. Today Morlaix is a delightful place. The old town

lies close to the feet of a giant granite viaduct astride the valley. Beyond the viaduct (walk across for excellent views), steep alleys trickle through a maze of churches and timbered buildings, some in an elaborate local style called 'lantern houses'. The **Maison de la Duchesse Anne** is the best of these while, the **Musée de Morlaix** is noted for its art exhibitions.

www.tourisme.morlaix.fr

🚪 6B 🍴 L'Hermine (€), 35 rue Ange de Guernisac, 02 98 88 10 91

🚌 Lannion, Roscoff, Carhaix–Plouguer etc 🚊 Roscoff, Lannion, Brest, St-Brieuc, Rennes

ℹ️ Place des Otages, 02 98 62 14 94

Maison de la Duchess Anne

✉️ 33 rue du Mur ☎️ 02 98 88 23 26; www.mda-morlaix.com 🕐 May–Sep Mon–Sat 11–6; closed Sun and Thu am in May 💷 Inexpensive

Musée de Morlaix

✉️ Place des Jacobins and 9 Grand'Rue ☎️ 02 98 88 68 88; www.musee.ville.morlaix.fr 🕐 Jul, Aug daily 10–12:30, 2–6:30; Apr, May, Sep Mon, Wed–Sat 10–12, 2–6, Sun 2–6; Oct–Mar, Jun 10–12, 2–5; closed Tue and Sun 💷 Inexpensive

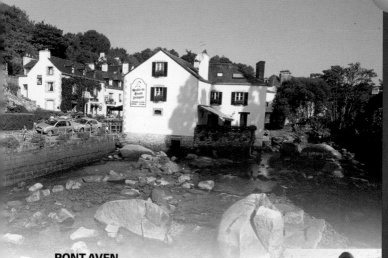

PONT-AVEN

Few of the watermills that once filled the town of Pont-Aven remain, but its picturesque riverside houses would still be recognizable to the painters who flocked here during the 19th century. The most notable member of the Pont-Aven School was Gauguin, though few of his works are on display in the **Musée Municipal des Beaux Arts.**

A wander through the old streets and nearby woods, however, will evoke many of the scenes he painted, notably the charming Chapelle de Trémalo, where a crucifix in the nave was the inspiration for his startling Christ Jaune. Pont-Aven's natural attractions are supplemented by good restaurants, hotels and shops.

www.pontaven.com

🚩 6F 🍴 Sur le Pont (€–€€€), 11 place Paul Gauguin, 02 98 06 16 16
🚌 Nos 14, 21 (Concarneau–Quimper) 🚢 Estuary cruises to Port-Manec'h
ℹ️ 5 place de l'Hôtel de Ville, 02 98 06 04 70

Musée Municipal des Beaux Arts

✉️ Place de l'Hôtel de Ville ☎ 02 98 06 14 43 🕐 Jul, Aug daily 10–7; Sep–Jun 10–12:30, 2–6; closed Jan 💰 Moderate

a drive 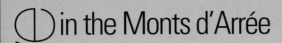 in the Monts d'Arrée

The village of Sizun makes a pleasant starting point.

Its church has elaborate panelled vaulting and decorated beams, and a parish close with a magnificent triumphal arch. The Maison de la Rivière and the Maison du Lac deal with aspects of the local waterways and their wildlife.

From Sizun, take the D764 eastwards, pausing at the Moulins de Kerouat after 3km (2 miles).

This restored mill complex of bake houses and outbuildings is now a museum of country life (Mar–Oct).

Continue on the same road to Commana.

The landscapes become wilder and the hills higher. The village of Commana has a fine church and an *allée couverte*.

East of Commana on the same road is the Roc'h Trévézel.

At 384m (1,260ft), this is one of the best viewpoints in Brittany, with views as far as Baie de Lannion on a clear day.

Take the D785 southwards, stopping at Montagne St-Michel after 13km (8 miles).

This is a slightly lower summit (380m/1,247ft), and can be reached by car. The surrounding ridge is the highest point in Brittany.

Continue 7km (4 miles) down the D785 to Brasparts.

Brasparts has a fine church and parish close. Inside the church is a lovely baroque altarpiece with blue and gold barleysugar columns decorated with vines and snakes.

Retrace the route for 2.5km (1.5 miles) northwards and take the D30 northwest to St-Rivoal.

This hamlet has an attractive *ecomusée*, the Maison Cornec (Jun–Sep). Wind westwards through the lanes to Ménez-Meur. This wildlife reserve and information centre is a good place to put the Armorique park in perspective.

Drive north up the D18 to return to Sizun.

Distance 60km (37 miles)
Time Allow a day if you want to see most of the sights and have a walk
Start/end point Sizun ✚ 5C
Lunch Restaurants are scarce, and most museums do not have coffee shops. Take a picnic with you or try Les Voyageurs (€–€€) in Sizun, ➤ 89

PRESQU'ÎLE DE CROZON

Best places to see, pages 50–51.

QUIMPER

Best places to see, pages 52–53.

ROSCOFF

Roscoff successfully combines the role of ferry port with that of seaside resort and export centre for vegetables and seafood. Thalassotherapy and seaweed research are other sidelines. The pretty, old fishing quarter remains intact despite the demands of modern shipping, but the bereted 'Onion Johnnies' who once loaded their wares on to bicycles for the ferry crossing have long since been replaced by refrigerated container juggernauts. In the old town, the main monument is the church of Notre-Dame-de-Kroaz-Batz, with one of Brittany's finest lantern bell towers. On the Pointe de

Bloscon, subtropical gardens flourish. A good excursion from Roscoff is the 15-minute boat-trip to the Île de Batz, with sandy beaches and another exotic garden.

www.roscoff-tourisme.com

✚ 6B 🍴 Le Surcouf (€–€€), 14 rue Amiral Réveillére, 02 98 69 71 89
🚌 Brest, Morlaix, Quimper 🚊 Morlaix 🚢 Brittany Ferries (Plymouth UK); trips to Île de Batz 🛈 Quai d'Auxerre, 02 98 61 12 13

ST-POL-DE-LÉON

During the Middle Ages, St-Pol was the religious centre of North Finistère. Its most memorable landmark is the magnificent belfry of the Kreisker Chapel, soaring 77m (253ft) high. Near by rise the rival twin spires of the Cathedral. Built of Norman limestone, the interior is full of fascinating details. What looks like an old stone bath tub (a Roman sarcophagus) serves as a stoup, and a little door below the right tower was used by lepers.

St-Pol is renowned as an agricultural centre of the fertile Golden Belt *(Ceinture d'Orée)* and all around the town early vegetables grow, particularly onions, artichokes, potatoes and cauliflowers. If you catch it on a Tuesday (market day) you will see it at its liveliest.
www.saintpoldeleon.fr

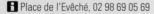 6B 🍴 Auberge Pomme d'Api (€€–€€€), 49 rue Verderel 🚌 🚆 Same services as Roscoff (see opposite)

ℹ Place de l'Evêché, 02 98 69 05 69

HOTELS

L'ABER WRAC'H
Baie des Anges (€€–€€€)
This stylish little seaside hotel and spa enjoys an entrancing location overlooking a calm sea inlet on the northwestern Côte des Abers. No restaurant, but room service is available.

✉ 350 route des Anges ☎ 02 98 04 90 04; www.baie-des-anges.com

🕐 Closed 10–20 Dec, mid-Jan to mid-Feb

BÉNODET
Armoric (€–€€€)
A welcoming, smartly refurbished hotel at the approach to the resort, with large gardens and a heated pool. Golf and thalassotherapy packages available.

✉ 3 rue de Penfoul ☎ 02 98 57 04 03; www.armoric-benodet.com

BREST
Hotel de la Corniche (€–€€)
Traditionally furnished, Breton-style house near the naval base. Tennis court and small gym plus great views/walks along the corniche or over the Recouvrance bridge into town.

✉ 1 rue Amiral Nico ☎ 02 98 45 12 42; www.hotel-la-corniche.com

CARANTEC
Carantec–Patrick Jeffroy (€€€)
Upmarket restaurant-with-rooms offering stunning views over the Baie de Morlaix. The chef-owner favours foie gras with seafood.

✉ 20 rue du Kelenn ☎ 02 98 67 00 47; www.hoteldecarantec.com

🕐 Closed end Nov to mid-Dec, last week Jan–first week Feb, Mon and Tue off-season

LE CONQUET
La Vinotière (€–€€€)
This small, stylish hotel whose 16th-century stone walls combine perfectly with contemporary wood and colourful textiles is named after a nearby lighthouse. Tearoom serves delicious cakes/pastries.

✉ 1 rue du Lieutenant Jourden ☎ 02 98 89 17 79; www.lavinotiere.com

CONCARNEAU
Hotel des Halles (€–€€)
The nautical-themed rooms in this cosy hotel near the *ville close* and beaches are all decorated differently. Organic pastries for breakfast and eco-friendly philosophy.

✉ Place del l'Hotel de Ville, rue Charles Linement ☎ 02 98 97 11 41; www.hoteldeshalles.com

DOUARNENEZ
Clos de Vallombreuse (€€)
Right in the heart of the old town, this secluded mansion has elegant, sophisticated furnishings and a noteworthy restaurant. The swimming pool overlooks the bay.

✉ 7 rue d'Étienne d'Orves ☎ 02 98 92 63 64; www.closvallombreuse.com

LANDERNEAU
Clos du Pontic (€–€€)
A quiet, well-equipped hotel in an unusual turreted building with modern extensions. The restaurant specializes in regional cooking.

✉ Rue du Pontic ☎ 02 98 21 50 91, www.clos-pontic.com

LOCQUIREC
Grand Hôtel des Bains (€€€)
Stylish belle époque hotel featuring one of the world's best spas. Great views and lovely coastal walks around the peninsula.

✉ 15 rue de l'Église ☎ 02 98 67 41 02; www.grand-hotel-des-bains.com

MORGAT
Julia (€–€€€)
A welcoming, family-run hotel on the Crozon peninsula, with bright, fresh decor and great home-cooking. Attractive circular, art-filled dining room.

✉ 43 rue du Tréflez ☎ 02 98 27 05 89; www.hoteljulia.fr

MORLAIX
Le Manoir Ker-Huella (€€)
TV-free bed-and-breakfast in a turreted, 19th-century *maison*

bourgeoise with all its original features. Kids will love the little Ouessant sheep and pygmy goats in the large garden.

✉ 78 Voie d'Accès aux Port ☎ 02 98 88 05 52

NÉVEZ
Ar Men Du (€€–€€€)

This small, smart hotel-restaurant has a wonderful coastal setting overlooking a tidal islet. Bedrooms are well equipped and contemporary; all have sea views. Very popular restaurant.

✉ Raguenez-Plage, Port Manec'h ☎ 02 98 06 84 22; www.men-du.com
🕐 Closed Nov to mid-Mar except Christmas, New Year

PONT-AVEN
Hôtel des Mimosas (€–€€)

A simple place at the far end of the harbour with waterfront views and a cosy, nautical-looking bistro. The menu features seafood.

✉ 22 square Théodore Botrel ☎ 02 98 06 00 30; www.hotels-pont-aven.com
🕐 Closed 11 Nov–15 Dec

QUIMPER
Best Western Hotel Kregenn (€€–€€€)

Some of the rooms in this chic, contemporary hotel have their own jacuzzi. Breakfast on the south-facing patio on warmer days or take tea in the Treizh bar post-sightseeing.

✉ 13 Rue des Réguaires ☎ 02 98 95 08 70; www.hotel-kregenn.fr

ROSCOFF
Le Brittany (€€€)

A tasteful, manor-house hotel with an indoor swimming pool and an excellent gourmet restaurant right by the sea.

✉ Boulevard Ste-Barbe ☎ 02 98 69 70 78; www.hotel-brittany.com
🕐 Closed mid-Nov to mid-Mar

Hôtel du Centre (€–€€)

Owned by the same family as Le Brittany, this budget option in the old port has cheerful contemporary rooms with stylish grey, white and red decor. Popular bar and restaurant.

✉ 5 rue Gambetta ☎ 02 98 61 24 25; www.chezjanie.com ◷ Closed mid-Nov to mid-Feb

STE-ANNE-LA-PALUD
La Plage (€€€)

Tranquil, upmarket hotel in an isolated beachside location. Enjoy the sunsets from the panoramic gourmet restaurant.

✉ Ste-Anne-la-Palud ☎ 02 98 92 50 12; www.plage.com ◷ Open Apr–Oct

STE-MARINE
Hotel du Bac (€€)

Just across the peaceful Odet estuary from lively Bénodet, this chic restaurant-with-rooms has bright, contemporary bedrooms and wonderful views. Terrace dining. Always very popular.

✉ 19 rue du Bac ☎ 02 98 51 33 33; www.hoteldubac.fr ◷ Closed mid-Nov to mid-Dec

TRÉGUNC
Les Grandes Roches (€€–€€€)

Just 3km (2 miles) east of Concarneau, this rambling old Breton house feels surprisingly rural in its extensive grounds dotted with rocks and menhirs. Swimming pool and gourmet restaurant.

✉ Rue des Grandes Roches ☎ 02 98 97 62 97 ◷ Closed Dec, Jan

RESTAURANTS

BREST
Le Ruffé (€–€€)

Great food and friendly service are the hallmarks of this gourmet restaurant near the train station. Try scallops au gratin followed by crème brulée with caramelized apples.

✉ 1 bis rue Yves Collet ☎ 02 98 46 07 70; www.le-ruffe.com ◷ Daily 12–3:30, 7–9.30, closed Sun eve and Mon

Ma Petite Folie (€–€€)

This former lobster boat is moored in the pleasure port and serves mainly fishy fare like grilled lobster and potted crab.

✉ Port de Plaisance ☎ 02 98 42 44 42 ◷ Daily 10–2, 7:30–9:30

CONCARNEAU
Chez Armande (€–€€€)
Unpretentious, family-run fish restaurant serving excellent menus from €15 at lunchtime. Try the *cotriade* – Breton fish stew

✉ 15 bis avenue Dr Nicolas ☎ 02 98 97 00 76 🕐 Daily 12–1:45, 7–9:45; closed 6–26 Nov, Tue Oct–Mar

L'Amiral (€–€€)
A smart, popular bar-restaurant overlooking the Ville Close, decorated in nautical style. Excellent seafood and good-value lunchtime menu.

✉ 1 avenue Pierre Guéguin ☎ 02 98 60 55 23; www.restaurant-amiral.com 🕐 Daily 9:30am–10:30pm; closed 28 Sep–12 Oct, Feb, school hols, Sun eve, Mon Oct–Apr

Le Pennti (€)
Flower-decked, stone house in the *ville close* serving up an award-winning selection of pancakes such as the *complet* (ham, egg and cheese). There is a characterful dining room along with a pretty garden terrace.

✉ 6 place St-Guénolé ☎ 02 98 97 46 02; www.creperie-lepennti.com 🕐 11:30–2:30, 6:30–9:30; closed Nov–Easter

LE CONQUET
Hostellerie de la Pointe St-Mathieu (€–€€€)
Elaborate seafood dishes are served in the stone dining room of this dramatically set hotel-restaurant facing the Atlantic. Stunning dessert trolley.

✉ Pointe St-Mathieu ☎ 02 98 89 00 19; www.pointestmathieu.com 🕐 Daily 12–1:30, 7:30–9; closed mid-Feb to mid-Mar; Sun eve Oct–Mar

Relais du Vieux Port (€)
Charming, breezily decorated harbourfront restaurant with rooms serving simple snacks, *crêpes*, salads, etc, as well as more substantial dishes like pan-fried scallops.

✉ 1 quai du Drellach ☎ 02 98 89 15 91; www.lerelaisduvieuxport.com 🕐 Daily 12–9; closed Jan

CROZON
Hostellerie de la Mer (€–€€€)
Reserve ahead at this hotel-restaurant for a quayside view of the Rade de Brest. Mainly fish menu specializing in Atlantic species.
✉ Le Fret ☎ 02 98 27 61 90; www.hostelleriedelamer.com ⏰ Daily 12:15–2, 7:15–9

Mutin Gourmand (€€–€€€)
You'll find whatever's freshest from the market at this hotel-restaurant. Accomplished seafood dishes such as buckwheat blinis topped with spider crab and langoustine.
✉ Hotel de la Presqu'île, place de l'Église ☎ 02 98 27 06 51; www.mutingourmand.fr ⏰ Closed Sun eve, Tue lunch Oct–Mar; last 3 weeks Mar and first 3 weeks Oct

GUIMILIAU
Ar Chupen (€)
Lacy *galettes* and *crêpes* with a wide choice of fillings in this old Breton farmhouse a short walk from the famous parish close. Artichokes are a speciality.
✉ 43 rue du Calvaire ☎ 02 98 68 73 63 ⏰ Daily 12–3; closed Sun–Fri eve except Jul, Aug

LOCRONAN
Ty Coz (€)
Charming *crêperie* and *glacier* in an old stone building on the main square. Try the *andouille de guémene* (chitterling sausage).
✉ Place de l'Église ☎ 02 98 91 70 79 ⏰ 12–8:45; closed Oct–Easter, Mon (except hols)

MORLAIX
L'Hermine (€)
A welcoming *crêperie* in a picturesque stone building on one of Morlaix's cobbled alleys. Rustic interior; pavement tables and late opening in summer. Smoked salmon and seaweed is a favourite.
✉ 35 rue Ange de Guernisac ☎ 02 98 88 10 91 ☎ Closed two weeks Jan and two weeks Apr

Marée Bleue (€–€€)

Traditional menu and interesting wines in an elegant, cosy restaurant in an alley just off Morlaix's main square. Tasty *kig ha farz* (Breton stew speciality).

✉ 3 rampe St-Mélaine ☎ 02 98 63 24 21 🕐 Daily 12–1:30, 7:30–9:30; closed Oct, Sun eve, Mon Oct–Mar

QUIMPER
La Fleur du Sel (€€)

A good place for lunch opposite the *faïenceries* factories in Locmaria, with waterfront views. Try the duck *confit* or roast lamb.

✉ 1 quai Neuf ☎ 02 98 55 04 71; www.fleur-de-sel-quimper.com 🕐 Daily 12–2, 7–9; closed Sat lunch, Sun lunch

RIEC-SUR-BÉLON
Chez Jacky (€–€€€)

Well-known fish-farming enterprise with on-site brasserie on the Bélon waterfront. Sample home-grown oysters, lobsters and other shellfish on sturdy picnic tables.

✉ Port de Bélon ☎ 02 98 06 90 32; www.chez-jacky.com 🕐 Tue–Sun 12–2, 7–9; closed Oct–Easter, Sun eve and Mon

ROSCOFF
Le Surcouf (€–€€)

Popular restaurant offering value-for-money menus with a heavy seafood accent. Enjoy sea bass with pink onions while checking out the lobsters and crabs in the large, glass tank.

✉ 14 rue Amiral Réveillère ☎ 02 98 69 71 89; www.jalima.fr 🕐 Tue–Thu 12–2, 6:30–9; closed Wed

ST-POL-DE-LÉON
Auberge la Pomme d'Api (€–€€€)

Acclaimed fine dining in a 16th-century setting. Elaborately named dishes using the local produce of the *Centure d'Orée* (Golden Belt) include Thai-style langoustines with lentils from St-Pol.

✉ 49 rue Verderel ☎ 02 98 69 04 36 🕐 Daily 12–2, 7–9:30; closed Sun eve, Mon off-season

ST-THÉGONNEC
Auberge St-Thégonnec (€€–€€€)
Chef Emmanuel Nivet uses the best regional produce at this smart hotel-restaurant. The chocolate dessert trio is to die for.

✉ 6 place de la Mairie ☎ 02 98 79 61 18; www.aubergesaintthegonnec.com
🕓 Daily 12–1:30, 7:30–9; closed mid-Dec to mid-Jan, Sun lunch Sep–Mar

SHOPPING

CRAFTS AND REGIONAL PRODUCTS
Algoplus
Seaweed is processed into many forms for culinary, cosmetic and pharmaceutical uses by this enterprising firm in the commercial harbour. Free guided tours of the plant from April to September.

✉ Port du Bloscon, Roscoff ☎ 02 98 61 14 14; www.algoplus-roscoff.fr

Comptoir de la Mer
This amazing chandlery stocks many items for leisure sailors and holidaymakers, including marine clothing and nauticalia.

✉ Port de Pêche, St-Guénolé ☎ 02 98 58 66 24 🕓 Mon–Sat 8–12, 2–6:30

Comptoir des Produits Bretons
This shop has one of the widest selections of Breton crafts and regional products, including seascapes, outdoor gear, jewellery.

✉ 3 quai de Cornouaille, Landerneau ☎ 02 98 21 35 93; www.comptoir-produits-bretons.com 🕓 Mon–Sat 9:30–12, 2–7, Sun 2–6:30

Faïencerie HB-Henriot
The largest and most high-profile local pottery firm, still using traditional hand-decoration methods and personally signed by the artist. Factory tours (some in English) show the process.

✉ Rue Haute, Locmaria, Quimper ☎ 02 98 90 09 36; www.hb-henriot.com

Keltia Musique
A wide selection of Breton and Celtic music recordings, books and instruments from France's leading Celtic music distributor.

✉ 1 place au Beurre, Quimper ☎ 02 98 95 42 65; www.keltiamusique.com
🕓 Mon–Sat 10–12:30, 2–7

Le Minor

This shop near the castle specializes in the town's local embroidery. Head upstairs for wall-hangings and household linen.

✉ 5 quai St-Laurent, Pont-l'Abbé ☎ 02 98 87 07 22; www.leminorboutique.com ⏱ Tue–Sat 9–12, 2–7

FOOD AND DRINK

Biscuiterie Traou Mad

One of many shops selling the town's speciality butter biscuits known as *galettes de Pont-Aven* in attractive tins.

✉ 10 place Gauguin, Pont-Aven ☎ 02 98 06 01 03; www.traoumad.com ⏱ May–Sep daily 8:45–7:30; Oct–Mar Mon–Sat 9:15–12:15, 2–7, Sun 10–12:30, 2:30–7

Chocolatier Chatillon

This *chocolatier* offers free tours to watch chocolates and biscuits being made, followed by tastings. Be sure to try the florentines.

✉ 46 place Charles de Gaulle, Pleyben ☎ 02 98 26 63 77; www.chatillon-chocolat.com ⏱ Mon–Sat 9–12:30, 2–7

Larnicol

An enticing cave-like shop in the *ville close* selling biscuits, chocolates and other goodies. Also in Auray, Quimper and Nantes.

✉ 9 rue Vauban, Concarneau ☎ 02 98 60 46 87; www.larnicol.com

ENTERTAINMENT

Le Ceili

A wide choice of beers, including local varieties, are sold in this Breton pub. Occasional concerts of Celtic music and sea shanties.

✉ 4 rue Aristide Briand, Quimper ☎ 02 98 95 17 61 ⏱ Mon–Sat 10:30am–1am, Sun 5pm–1am.

The Tara Inn

Welcoming Irish pub in Brest's port. Live music Thursday evenings and Irish dancing on the first Sunday of the month at 3pm.

✉ 1 rue Blaveau, Brest ☎ 02 98 80 36 07 ⏱ Mon–Fri 11am–1pm, Sat–Sun 3pm–1am

Côtes d'Armor

Few visitors would dispute that the coastline of Côtes d'Armor is the most dramatically beautiful in Brittany. Highlights are the Emerald and Pink Granite coasts, where its northerly peninsulas meet the sea in a spectacular series of headlands, cliffs, bizarre rock formations and scattered islands.

Dinan

Added blessings are its charming old towns (Dinan, Tréguier, Lannion, Paimpol). In summer, its main centres and hotels can become crowded, but nowhere except perhaps St-Brieuc feels overpoweringly urban, and it's never impossible to find a secluded beach.

Some areas have fascinating historic associations: the Côte de Goëlo south of Paimpol was a centre of Resistance operations during World War II. Its less well-known interior, startlingly empty in parts, is worth exploring too. As you travel westwards through Côtes d'Armor towards Basse-Bretagne (Lower Brittany), the Breton character becomes steadily more pronounced and Breton place names appear on signposts.

CAP FRÉHEL

This spectacular promontory consists of gnarled grey cliffs of schist and sandstone streaked with red porphyry rising to a height of 70m (230ft) above a sea of jade. Best views are from the sea; summer excursion boats tour the coast from St-Malo and Dinard. The road approach leads through moorland and pine forests, with parking space at the square-towered **lighthouse.** Views extend to Bréhat, St-Malo and the Channel Isles on clear days, and in misty conditions, a foghorn sounds at intervals. Seabirds crowd on the fissured Fauconnière rocks (a nature reserve). Walks around the cape, past aged cannons rusting in a froth of sea-pinks and white campion, are exceptionally beautiful. Take binoculars and a camera.

www.pays-de-frehel.com

✚ 12B 🍴 Le Victorine (€–€€), place de Chambly, Fréhel, 02 96 41 55 55
🚌 02 to Fréhel from St-Brieuc, Lamballe, Erquy, Le Val-André 🚢 Boat trips from several Emerald Coast resorts
ℹ Place de Chambly, Fréhel, 02 96 41 53 81

Phare du Cap Fréhel (lighthouse)

☎ 02 96 41 53 81 🕐 Apr–Aug Wed–Mon 12:30–6, Tue 1:30–6; Sep Fri–Mon 2–5 ✋ Inexpensive

CÔTE D'EMERAUDE

The Emerald Coast lies between the Pointe de Grouin (north of Cancale), and Le Val-André – a stretch of rocky headlands, sandy bays, estuaries, capes and islets. West of St-Malo and Dinard

stretches a long string of small resorts, many named after saints and all with lovely sandy beaches – Sables-d'Or-les-Pins and Le Val-André have two of the best. St-Cast-le-Guildo and Le Val-André are the largest and best equipped holiday resorts. East of Cap Fréhel (opposite) stands Fort la Latte, a romantic coastal fortress (➤ below). The Baie de la Frenaye is renowned for mussel farming, while Erquy specializes in scallops.

✚ 12B

CÔTE DE GRANIT ROSE
Best places to see, pages 42–43.

DINAN
Best places to see, pages 44–45.

FORT LA LATTE
This privately owned coastal fortress stands on a rocky promontory severed from the mainland by chasms forming a natural tidal moat, and is entered by a drawbridge. The present structure dates back mainly to the 14th century, but was extensively renovated by Louis XIV's military architect Vauban at the end of the 17th century. The fort is best known as a location in the 1958 film *The Vikings*, starring Kirk Douglas and Tony Curtis.

www.castlelalatte.com

✚ 12B ✉ Plévenon–Fréhel ☎ 02 96 41 57 11 🕐 Apr–Sep daily 10–12:30, 2–6 (Jul, Aug 10–7); rest of year Sat, Sun and school hols 2–6 ▮ Moderate

ÎLE DE BRÉHAT

Bréhat, about 2km (1.2 miles) north of Paimpol, consists of two main islands linked by a bridge. Beaches of pink granite fringe the indented coastline. The northern island is wilder and less crowded, while the southern island is scattered with elegant villas and subtropical gardens, and contains Bréhat's main community Le Bourg. Here you can visit the Moulin à Marée du Birlot, a restored 17th-century windmill (open Jun–Aug weekends, depending on tide). Cars are banned, but Bréhat is criss-crossed by paths, and small enough to walk or cycle across in an hour.

www.ile-de-brehat.com

✚ 9A 🍴 La Vieille Auberge (€–€€), 02 96 20 00 24 ⛴ Cruises and ferries from Pointe de l'Arcouest, Erquy, Binic, St-Quay-Portrieux
ℹ La Mairie, Le Bourg, 02 96 20 04 15

LAMBALLE

France's second largest **Haras National** (national stud farm) is in the inland town of Lamballe. An imposing stable-block in extensive grounds just northwest of Lamballe's historic centre provides quarters for around 70 stallions, plus a number of riding horses. The most notable breed is the beefy Breton draught horse, once used for ploughing and cart-pulling, but they share their stalls with fine-boned thoroughbreds, saddle horses and Irish Connemaras.

Lamballe presides over an agricultural area, and much of its business is related to its role as market centre for the Penthièvre region. Modern suburbs sprawl in all directions, but its most attractive part is the old quarter around the place du Martray, a compact cluster of noteworthy churches and picturesque timbered houses. One of the most striking of these, the Maison du Bourreau (the Hangman's House), is home to the **Musée Mathurin-Méheut** and the **Musée du Pays de Lamballe.** One is an informative local folk and history exhibition; the other displays watercolours, drawings and ceramics by the artist Mathurin Méheut, who was born in Lamballe in 1882.

www.lamballe-tourisme.com

🚏 11C 🍴 Restaurants and pubs in old town, such as La Tour des Archants, rue Dr Lavergne (€€) 🚌 CAT Lines 01 (St-Cast-le-Guildo), 03 (St-Brieuc) HSNCF links to Dinan, St-Brieuc, Rennes ❓ Equestrian events all summer

🛈 Entrance to Haras National, 02 96 31 05 38

Haras National

✉ Place du Champ de Foire ☎ 02 96 50 06 98; www.haraspatrimoine.com
🕐 Jul–Sep several visits daily; Oct–Jun Tue–Sun 3pm ✋ Moderate

Musée Mathurin-Méheut

✉ Maison du Bourreau ☎ 02 96 31 19 99 🕐 Jun–Sep Mon–Sat 10–12, 2:30–6; May, Oct–Dec Wed, Fri, Sat 2:30–5; Apr Mon–Sat 10–12, 2:30–5
✋ Inexpensive (joint ticket available)

Musée du Pays de Lamballe

✉ Maison du Bourreau ☎ 02 96 34 77 63 🕐 Jun–Sep Tue–Sat 10–12, 2:30–6 ✋ Inexpensive (joint ticket available)

LANNION

This attractive port acts is the administrative centre of the Trégor region. A strategic bridging point and route hub, it gets crowded on market day (Thursday), but is a lively and enjoyable shopping centre. Long wharves and towpaths fringe the waterfront, and fishing boats give the town a seaside air, though it is some distance inland. The lower town is a well-preserved assembly of old gabled houses. Two prominent churches catch the eye on either side of the river: the monastery of Ste-Anne on the west bank and St-Jean-du-Baly in the centre. The most interesting church, Brélévenez, crowns the hill to the north of town and can be reached via a flight of 142 steps, or less arduously by a circuitous road. Founded by 12th-century Templars, it displays a mixture of styles. The Romanesque apse is a maze of pillars and ornately carved capitals, and the crypt below contains a fine Entombment.

Lannion makes a good excursion base. The Léguer estuary and the wooded valleys inland offer excellent touring. Half a dozen châteaux lie within easy reach, including the stately ruins of Tonquédec and Coatfrec, inhabited Kergrist (gardens open) and richly furnished Rosanbo.

www.ot-lannion.fr

🚌 8B 🍴 La Ville Blanche (€€–€€€), on the D786, 02 96 37 04 28 🚍 Lines 6 (Guingcamp), 7 (Paimpol), 15 (Pink Granite Coast), 30 (Morlaix) 🚆 Morlaix, Guingamp ❓ Kayaking and rafting at the white-water stadium Base Nautique de Lannion ☎ 02 96 37 43 90 ℹ️ 2 quai d'Aiguillon, 02 96 46 41 00

Tricolaine

PAIMPOL

Paimpol's traditional way of life for centuries was cod fishing in the perilous waters of Newfoundland and Iceland. Today's trawlers stay closer inshore, and oyster farming in the Trieux estuary has brought new wealth, but the **Musée de la Mer** (Maritime Museum) contains many fascinating reminders of the cod industry. The place du Martray is the focal point. Surrounded by charming old houses, it holds a thriving fish and produce market.

Paimpol lacks good sandy beaches, but makes a fine touring base. Pointe de l'Arcouest, to the north, is the ferry terminal for the Île de Bréhat (➤ 108). Southwards lies the Côte de Goëlo, and the impressive ruins of the 13th-century Abbaye de Beauport (www.abbaye-beauport.com). A scenic route near Plouha takes in Plage Bonaparte, scene of several daring escapes from occupied France during World War II. Inland, the church at Kermaria-an-Iskuit contains a *danse macabre* fresco.

www.paimpol goclo.com

✚ 9B 🍴 La Vieille Tour (€–€€), 13 rue de L'Église, 02 96 20 83 18 🚌 Lines 9 (St-Brieuc), 7 (Lannion)

ℹ Place de La Républic, 02 96 20 83 16

Musée de la Mer

✉ Rue de Labenne ☎ 02 96 22 02 19 🕐 Jun–Aug daily 10:30–12:30, 2–6:30; Apr, May, Sep 2–6 ♿ Moderate

PERROS-GUIREC

The Pink Granite Coast's largest resort has two splendid beaches, a
casino, thalassotherapy centre and modern marina, though the
town has no special Breton charm or architectural distinction apart
from the church of St-Jacques, with a spiky belfry and trefoil porch.
Boat trips to the bird sanctuary at Les Sept Îles (➤ opposite) are
popular. Don't miss the watchpath walk to Ploumanac'h past the
most spectacular section of the Pink Granite Coast (➤ 42–43).

www.perros-guirec.com

✚ 8A 🍴 Au Bon Accueil (€–€€€), 11 rue Landerval, 02 96 23 25 77

🚌 Line 15 (Lannion, Trégastel, Trébeurden, Pleumeur-Bodou)

🛈 21 place de l'Hôtel de Ville, 02 96 23 21 15

PLEUMEUR-BODOU

From a distance, a huge white golfball seems to have been left on
the heathlands northwest of Lannion. This was once the nerve-
centre of France's advanced telecommunications research. It now
houses the **Cité des Télecoms,** an exhibition on long-distance
message-relay from early semaphore to the latest technology.
There's also a **Planétarium** and **Le Village Gaulois** (➤ 69).

www.pleumeur-bodou.com

✚ 7A

Cité des Télecoms

✉ Site de Cosmopolis ☎ 02 96 46 63 80; www.leradome.com 🕐 Jul, Aug

daily 10–7; Apr, Sep Mon–Fri 10–6 🖐 Moderate 🍽 On-site cafes (€)
🚌 Line 15 (Perros-Guirec, Lannion and Pink Granite resorts)

Planétarium

✉ Site de Cosmopolis ☎ 02 96 15 80 32; www.planetarium-bretagne.fr
🕐 See website or telephone for show times 🖐 Moderate

Le Village Gaulois

✉ Site de Cosmopolis ☎ 02 96 91 83 95 🕐 Jul, Aug daily 10:30–7;
Apr–Jun, Sep Sun–Fri 2–6; closed Oct–Easter 🖐 Moderate

LES SEPT ÎLES

The seven scraps of land visible from the coast around Perros-Guirec are one of Brittany's most important bird sanctuaries, home to many species, including petrels and puffins. One island, Rouzic, is noted for a large colony of breeding gannets. Half-day boat trips from Ploumanac'h and Perros-Guirec (➤ opposite) sail all round the islands. Landings are permitted only on Île aux Moines, which has a ruined fortress and an old gunpowder factory.

✚ 8A ⛴ Gare Maritime de Perros-Guirec ☎ 02 96 91 10 00; www.armor-decouverte.fr 🕐 Feb–Nov

TRÉGASTEL

This popular family resort has some of the strangest of the Pink Granite Coast's rock formations. One extraordinary cluster has

been turned into an **aquarium** of local and Mediterranean species (tel: 02 96 23 48 58). Near by, a large indoor waterpark called Forum (tel: 02 96 15 30 44) has several pools maintained at a comfortable 28°C (82°F). Behind is the main beach of Plage de Coz-Pors. More intriguing rocks lie stranded at low tide on Grève Blanche. **www**.ville-tregastel.fr

✚ 7A 🍽 Le Macareux (€€–€€€), 21 rue des Plages Landrellec 🚌 Line 15 (Lannion–Perros-Guirec)
ℹ Place Ste-Anne, 02 96 15 38 38

a walk from Perros-Guirec

The coastguard's watchpath by the seashore from Perros-Guirec leads past an astonishing wilderness of rose-tinted boulders weathered into curious shapes. The coppery pink colours are particularly amazing at sunset.

From Perros-Guirec the path begins at Plage de Trestraou, hugging the shore beneath the cliffs.

At first it is pleasant but unspectacular, with views of Les Sept Îles and claw-like headlands. At Pors Rolland the rocks suddenly change gear, revealing weird, organic forms strewn chaotically over the seafront like unclaimed suitcases. The most peculiar of all are located in an orderly conservation zone or 'municipal park', where each formation is given some fanciful name (the Tortoise, the Armchair, etc). At the Maison du Littoral on the edge of the municipal park the emphasis is strictly on environmental care: *'La vie est fragile – ne brisez-la!'* A small display on local geology and natural history is housed inside.

Follow the rocks past the lighthouse round to Plage St-Guirec, where an oratory and a statue mark the local patron saint.

This Celtic monk arrived from Welsh shores in the 6th century and obviously appreciated the scenery. His talents ranged from curing abscesses, mentally handicapped children and fiery tempers to an occasional spot of marriage guidance counselling.

In Ploumanac'h, notice the eye-catching Château du Diable, an outcrop of granite rocks in the bay. This is where Henryk Sienkiewicz wrote Quo Vadis? at the turn of the 20th century. He was awarded the Nobel prize for literature in 1905.

Distance 6km (4 miles)
Time About 90 mins each way
Start point Perros-Guirec 🚏 8A
End point Ploumanac'h 🚏 7A
Lunch Take a picnic

TRÉGUIER

The historic town of Tréguier occupies a hilly site on the Jaudy estuary. Its most famous resident was Yves, the patron saint of lawyers. The cathedral is Tréguier's most impressive building, a mainly Gothic construction of pink granite. The great spire at its west end is a masterpiece of the Decorated period, pierced with multi-patterned holes to reduce wind resistance. Inside lies St Yves' tomb, flanked by votive candles. On the anniversary of his death on 19 May, a

pardon is held here. Outside the cathedral is place du Martray, surrounded by lovely old buildings. Near the tourist office is a poignant war memorial of a woman in Breton dress grieving for lost menfolk.

www.ville-treguier.fr

✚ 8A 🍴 Aigue Marine (€€), 5 rue Berthelot, 02 96 92 97 00

🚌 Line 7 (Lannion–Paimpol), 16 (Lannion–Plougrescant)

❓ Mid-May: Pardon de St-Yves

ℹ 67 rue Ernest Renan, 02 96 92 22 33

HOTELS

BRÉLIDY
Château de Brélidy (€€–€€€)
Elegantly renovated 16th-century manor set in extensive grounds.
There's river fishing available for keen anglers.
✉ Brélidy ☎ 02 96 95 69 38; www.chateau-brelidy.com ⏰ Closed
Jan–Easter

DINAN
D'Avaugour (€€–€€€)
A stylish hotel on the main square with gardens stretching over
the castle ramparts. Enjoy an aperitif on the flower-filled terrace.
✉ 1 place du Champ ☎ 02 96 39 07 49; www.avaugourhotel.com
⏰ Closed mid-Nov to mid-Feb

ERQUY
Beauséjour (€)
This reliable, flower-decked *Logis* has sea views and appetizing
regional food – *coquille St Jacques* is the house speciality.
✉ 21 rue de la Corniche ☎ 02 96 72 30 39; www.beausejour-erquy.com
⏰ Closed mid-Nov to mid-Mar; restaurant closed Mon Oct–Apr

ÎLE DE BREHAT
Bellevue (€€)
Idyllic little place near the harbour, with simple, fresh bedrooms
and a panoramic seafood restaurant. The 'Relaxation Package'
includes dinner, bed-and-breakfast and a day's bicycle hire.
✉ Port Clos ☎ 02 96 20 00 05; www.hotel-bellevue-brehat.com
⏰ Closed mid-Nov to Christmas and most of Jan to mid-Feb

LAMBALLE
Le Manoir des Portes (€€)
Charming hotel in a 16th-century stone house where the
bedrooms are furnished in a bright, contemporary style. The
restaurant is renowned for its traditional, seasonal menus.
✉ La Poterie ☎ 02 96 31 13 62; www.manoirdesportes.com ⏰ Closed
Christmas to New Year

PAIMPOL
Les Agapanthes (€)
Lovely 18th-century granite village house with views over to Bréhat island. The bright, fresh rooms are individually decorated.

✉ 1 rue Adrien Rebours, Ploubazlanec ☎ 02 96 55 89 06; www.hotel-les-agapanthes.com 🕐 Closed Jan

PERROS-GUIREC
Manoir du Sphinx (€€€)
An elegant turn-of-the-20th-century building in a spectacular cliff-top location. The charming bedrooms are beautifully furnished.

✉ 67 chemin de la Messe ☎ 02 96 23 25 42; www.lemanoirdusphinx.com 🕐 Closed mid-Jan to late Feb and last 2 weeks Nov

PLOUËR-SUR-RANCE
Manoir de Rigourdaine (€–€€)
A rambling country house in a rural setting overlooking the Rance. Elegant bedrooms in converted courtyard buildings. No restaurant.

✉ Route de Langrolay ☎ 02 96 86 89 96; www.hotel-rigourdaine.fr 🕐 Closed mid-Nov to Mar

SABLES-D'OR-LES-PINS
Le Manoir St-Michel (€–€€)
Traditionally furnished stone manor right next to the beach. Enjoy breakfast overlooking the hotel's lake on warmer days.

✉ 38 rue de la Carquois, Fréhel ☎ 02 96 41 48 87; www.fournel.de 🕐 Closed Nov–Mar

ST-CAST-LE-GUILDO
Port Jacquet (€)
Charming stone-built hotel high above the port with bright bedrooms and good cooking. Sea views and a warm welcome.

✉ 32 rue du Port ☎ 02 96 41 97 18; www.port-jacquet.com

TRÉBEURDEN
Ti al Lannec (€€€)
Child-friendly luxury hotel in a wonderful Pink Granite Coast

location. Welcoming owners, elegant decor and beautiful grounds.

✉ 14 allée de Mezo Guen ☎ 02 96 15 01 01; www.tiallannec.com
🕐 Closed Nov to mid-Mar

TRÉGUIER
Aigue Marine (€€)

A spacious modern hotel by the marina. Light, airy bedrooms, good leisure facilities, an excellent restaurant, delicious breakfasts.

✉ Port de Plaisance ☎ 02 96 92 97 00; www.aiguemarine.fr 🕐 Closed Jan to mid-Feb

LE VAL-ANDRE
Grand Hôtel du Val-André (€€–€€€)

A glorious seafront location and attractive grounds. Spacious, comfortable rooms and courteous management.

✉ 80 rue Amiral Charner ☎ 02 96 72 20 56; www.grand-hotel-val-andre.fr
🕐 Closed Jan

RESTAURANTS

DINAN
Auberge du Pelican (€€)

Tasty regional dishes served up in a smart dining room. Try fish soup to start followed by chicken in a creamy cider sauce.

✉ 3 rue Haute Vuie ☎ 02 96 39 47 05 🕐 Daily 12–2, 7–10; closed Mon and Thu eve (except Jul, Aug)

Café Terrasses (€–€€)

This all-day bistro overlooking the port offers a range of well-prepared dishes. Salads, omelettes and mussels are favourites.

✉ 2–4 rue du Quai ☎ 02 96 39 09 60 🕐 Daily 12–2, 7–9 (10 in summer); closed mid-Nov to mid-Dec, Jan and Sun eve, Mon, Tue eve Sep–Jun

Crêperie Ahna (€)

Meat cooked on sizzling stones as well as pancakes are on offer. Try the *Langueux* – chitterling sausage soaked in muscadet.

✉ 7 rue de la Poissonnerie ☎ 02 96 39 09 13 🕐 Daily 12–2:30, 7–10; closed Sun (except Jul–Aug)

ERQUY
L'Escurial (€€)
This is one of the best restaurants in the area. Scallops are a
speciality. Try them marinaded in salt crystals and spicy cream.
✉ Boulevard de la Mer ☎ 02 96 72 31 56 🕐 Daily 12–1:45, 7:30–9; closed
Jan, Sun eve, Thu eve and Mon (except Jul, Aug)

LAMBALLE
La Tour des Arc'hants (€€)
Cosy restaurant dating from the 14th century offering oysters from
Cancale, pan-fried duck and a Normandy apple tart with custard.
✉ 2 rue Dr Lavergne ☎ 02 96 31 01 37 🕐 Daily 12–1:30, 7–9; closed Sun
eve, Mon

MÛR-DE-BRETAGNE
Auberge Grand'Maison (€–€€€)
A gastronomic place of pilgrimage by Lac de Guerlédan. Excellent
value lunch menu. Reserve rooms if you want to stop over.
✉ 1 rue Léon-le-Cerf ☎ 02 96 28 51 10; www.auberge-grand-maison.com
🕐 Daily 12:30–1:30, 7:30–8:30; closed mid- to late Feb, most of Oct, Sun eve,
Mon, Tue lunch Nov–Apr

PAIMPOL
La Vieille Tour (€–€€€)
There's a good-value lunch menu in this stylish 16th-century inn.
Fish lovers will enjoy the cod fillet on smoked herring purée, while
a licorice-flavoured *bavarois* will tempt the sweet-toothed.
✉ 13 rue de l'Église ☎ 02 96 20 83 18 🕐 Daily 12:15–1:30, 7:30-9:30;
closed two weeks Jun, Mon, Sun eve and Wed eve (except Jul, Aug)

PERROS-GUIREC
Au Bon Accueil (€–€€€)
Let the sea air stimulate your taste buds in this light and airy
modern dining room overlooking the harbour. Traditional menu with
the emphasis on seafood.
✉ 11 rue Landerval ☎ 02 96 23 25 77 🕐 Daily 12:15–1:30, 7:30–9; closed
Sun eve and Mon (except Jul, Aug)

PLOUMANAC'H
Coste Mor (€–€€)
Despite the name, the food is inexpensive and the dining room faces one of Brittany's most dazzling seascapes. The seaside terrace is as good a place as any to tuck into a seafood platter.

✉ Hôtel St-Guirec, plage de St-Guirec ☎ 02 96 91 65 55; www.hotelsaint-guirec.com 🕑 Daily 12–2, 7–9; closed mid-Nov to Mar

ST-BRIEUC
Aux Pesked (€–€€)
A sophisticated modern restaurant on the hill leading down to the port. The emphasis is on local produce like pork with white beans.

✉ 59 rue du Légué ☎ 02 96 33 34 65; www.auxpesked.com 🕑 Daily 12:15–1:30, 7:30–9; closed early Jan, one week in May, one week in Sep, Sat lunch, Sun eve, Mon

LE VAL-ANDRÉ
Au Biniou (€€)
A well-known local favourite serving interesting seafood dishes in traditional surroundings. The langoustine skewers are very popular.

✉ 121 rue Clemenceau 🕑 02 96 72 24 35 🕑 Daily 12:30–2, 7:30–9:30; closed Feb, Tue Wed off-season

SHOPPING

ANTIQUES
In the port of Dahouët, near Le Val-André, several of the old sail-lofts on the quayside are now *brocantes* or antique stores.

Comptoirs de l'Ouest
An Aladdin's cave of bric-a-brac and second-hand goods crammed into a barn-like junk shop.

✉ Port de Dahouët 🕑 02 96 63 18 84 🕑 Thu–Sun 10:30–12:30, 2–6

ARTS AND CRAFTS
Dinan is one of the best places to look for regional products. Many of the ancient buildings on the steep street leading down to the port are now craft studios or galleries.

Angora de France

See how the rabbits are raised and inspect the clothes and accessories made from their silky wool.

✉ Château de Coat-Carric, Plestin-les-Grèves ☎ 02 96 35 62 49
🕐 Mon–Fri 2–6

Tannerie de Callac

Fish skin is a speciality at this leatherware outlet southwest of Guingamp. It sells belts, wallets, gloves, handbags and luggage.

✉ ZA de Kerguiniou, Callac ☎ 02 96 45 50 68; www.tannerie-de-callac.com
🕐 Mon–Tue 2–6

FOOD AND DRINK

Les Gavottes

This appetizing little shop sells speciality biscuits and sweets, including *gavottes* – a crisp, wafer-like version of *crêpes dentelles*.

✉ 9 rue du Château, Locmaria ☎ 02 96 87 06 48; www.locmaria.fr
🕐 Daily 10–6

ENTERTAINMENT

A la Truye qui File

At the sign of the spinning sow, this inn occupies a fine old medieval building in a cobbled alley locally nicknamed 'Thirsty Street' because of its lively bars. Blues, jazz and regional beers.

✉ 14 rue de la Cordonnerie, Dinan ☎ 02 96 39 72 29 🕐 Tue–Sun 11am–1am

Café Theodore

An old stone house west of Lannion offers local produce plus Breton and world music for an authentic evening out.

✉ Kerguerwen ☎ 02 96 35 29 40 🕐 Mon, Tue, Thu, Fri 9am–2pm, 5:30pm–1am, Sat 9am–1am, Sun 11am–11pm; closed Wed

Le Pub

This piano bar and disco pub near the harbour puts on a varied range of music and appeals to a wide age group.

✉ 3 rue des Islandais, Paimpol ☎ 02 96 20 82 31; www.lepub-paimpol.fr
🕐 Jul, Aug Tue–Sun 9pm–5am; Sep–Jun Thu–Sun 11pm–4am

Ille-et-Vilaine

This easterly *département* in Haute-Bretagne has two of Brittany's best-known towns: the popular ferry port of St-Malo, and the stylish resort of Dinard. It has hardly any of Brittany's rugged coastline, yet is by no means devoid of scenery and sightseeing. Don't miss the grand fortresses of Fougères, Combourg and Vitré that once protected the independent Duchy from its jealous French sister. The Breton capital, Rennes, deserves a day or two's exploration. And slip briefly across the Norman border for a look at one of France's greatest sights, the island abbey of Mont-St-Michel.

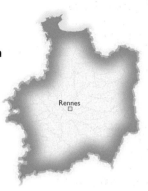

Rennes

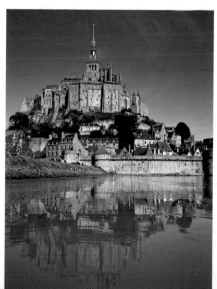

The brief stretch of coast between the river Rance and Normandy consists of flat, brackish saltmarshes. Southwards carve the sluggish waterways that give the *département* its name, linking the Channel with the Atlantic and saving fair-weather sailors the anxiety of negotiating Finistère's treacherous coastline.

CANCALE

Cancale is renowned for its oysters. The grey shoreline is covered with the shallow concrete beds *(parcs)* where they mature. After harvesting and cleaning, they are piled high on local stalls, or at the seafood restaurants along the waterfront in La Houle.

Just south of the port lies **La Ferme Marine,** an oyster farm and museum devoted to the life and times of the local mollusc (guided tours). After an introductory film show, visitors are shown the oyster beds and the workshops where washing, grading and packing take place. A restored *bisquine* (oyster boat) is now used for pleasure trips.

www.cancale-tourisme.fr

✚ 13B 🍴 Les Cancalais (€–€€), 12 quai Gambetta, 02 99 89 61 93

🚌 St-Malo to Mont-St-Michel

ℹ 44 rue du Port, 02 99 89 63 72

La Ferme Marine

✉ Plage de l'Aurore ☎ 02 99 89 69 99; www.ferme-marine.com

🕐 Jul–15 Sep daily 2pm (in English); mid-Feb to Oct Mon–Fri 3pm (in French)

✋ Moderate

COMBOURG

The massive 11th-century castle by the lakeshore, all crenellations and pepperpot towers, is the main focus of attention in this small town. Literary visitors have an additional interest in the building: the **castle** was the home of René de Chateaubriand, who wrote of his miserable childhood in the haunted bedroom.

www.combourg.org

✚ 14D 🍴 L'Ecrivain (€€), place St-Gilduin 🚌 11 (Rennes)

🚆 St-Malo–Rennes

ℹ Place Albert Parent, 02 99 73 13 93

Château de Combourg

 23 rue des Princes ☎ 02 99 73 22 95;
www.combourg.net ⚙ Guided tours: Jul,
Aug daily 10:30, 11:15, 2–5:30; Apr–Jun, Sep
Sun–Fri 2–5:30; Oct Sun–Fri 2–5. Park:
Apr–Sep 9:30–12:30, 2–6; Oct 10–12, 2–5
✋ Moderate

DINARD

This fashionable seaside resort was a
mere fishing village until the mid-19th
century. The sheltered climate and
setting attracted wealthy visitors who
built ornate villas on the wooded cliffs
above three sandy beaches (best
admired from the Promenade du Clair-
de-Lune). Holiday homes, yachts and
striped beach huts jostle along the
seafront. Dinard's excellent facilities
include an Olympic-sized swimming
pool, a casino, the modern Palais des
Arts et Festivals and boat trips up the
Rance and along the Emerald Coast.
Regattas, tennis tournaments, bridge
and afternoon tea punctuate the social
calendar. On the Rance estuary, south
of Dinard, is the world's first tidal
power station (➤ 139).
www.ot-dinard.com

✚ 13C 🍴 Didier Méril (€€), 1 place Général
de Gaulle, 02 99 46 95 74 🚌 16 (St-
Malo–Emerald Coast), 7a (Rennes) ⛴ Ferry
to St-Malo; cruises to Dinan; coastal trips
ℹ 2 boulevard Féart, 02 99 46 94 12

DOL-DE-BRETAGNE

Dol stands on the remains of a cliff amid low-lying pastureland reclaimed from the sea. The surrounding fields are famous for the prized *pré-salé* lamb raised here. Dol was founded in the 6th century by St Samson, one of Brittany's 'founding saints'. Its gaunt granite cathedral still dominates the town. A former school beside the cathedral houses an ambitious exhibition on medieval cathedrals, and the construction methods used during the period, called **Médiévalys,** which also houses exhibitions on knights and life in the Middle Ages. The explanatory labels to the models, diagrams and photographs have been translated into English but are rather technical. Several streets of picturesque timbered houses dating from the Middle Ages lie near by.

Just north of the town, the Mont-Dol, a granite mound topped by an ancient chapel, erupts suddenly from the saltmarsh plains, offering extensive views of the surrounding countryside. A legend declares this is the site of St Michael's apocalyptic struggle with Satan, and if you let your imagination run away with you, it is just about possible to spot St Michael's footprint in a clifftop rock by the chapel.

www.pays-de-dol.com

✚ 14C 🍴 La Cour Verte (€–€€), route de Rennes, 02 99 48 41 41 🚌 Line 17 (Mont-St-Michel, St-Malo, Fougéres) 🚆 Caen, Dinan, St-Malo, Rennes
ℹ Place de la Cathédrale, 02 99 48 15 37

Médiévalys

✉ Place de la Cathédrale ☎ 02 99 48 35 30 🕐 Jul, Aug daily 10–8; Apr–Jun, Sep, Oct 10–7; Nov–Mar 10–6 💰 Moderate

FOUGÈRES

Fougères is a frontier town, former capital of the swampy Marches dividing France and Brittany. For Victor-Hugo it was 'the Carcassonne of the North'. Its dominant feature is its castle (➤ 40–41), set in a tight loop of the River Nançon. The rocky spurs above the castle walls cradle the upper town of mostly 18th-century buildings – a stiff climb from the riverbank. Precipitous steps and alleys lead from the back of St-Léonard's church down to a much older sector around the place du Marchix, where tanneries and mills can be seen among a cluster of stone and half-timbered 16th century houses, dominated by the slender spire of St-Sulpice.

Fougères grew wealthy, like many Breton towns, on the textile trades of wool and hemp. Later it turned to shoe manufacture, supplemented by post-war ventures into electronics and robotics. Northeast of Fougères, beyond uninspiring modern suburbs, extends a state forest of beech, spruce and chestnut.

www.ot-fougeres.fr

✚ 16D 🍴 Restaurants and cafes in upper town, such as Crêperie Tivabro, place du Marchix (€) or in the old quarter around the castle 🚌 Line 9 Rennes, 17 St-Malo, 14 Vitré
ℹ 2 rue Nationale, 02 99 94 12 20

a walk around old Fougères

Head for the upper town and park in one of the squares near the tourist office. From here, walk along the pedestrianized rue Nationale.

Notice the elegant 14th-century belfry behind the covered market. Further along, a picturesque jettied and porticoed 16th-century house contains a museum dedicated to the Impressionist painter Emmanuel de la Villéon (1858–1944), a native of Fougères. About 100 of his drawings and watercolours (mostly local scenes) are displayed inside. Near the end of the street stands the church of St-Léonard by the Renaissance town hall. Behind the church, which dates from the 16th century, neatly kept municipal gardens give a splendid terrace vantage point over plunging wooded chasms, the mellow, brown-beamed houses of the Marchix quarter and the tremendous fortress below.

Using these as your target, thread your way down the stepped alleys and across the river via rue des Tanneurs.

The streets around the place du Marchix contain many ancient buildings. Gothic St-Sulpice church, built in Flamboyant style, contains fine 18th-century woodwork, 15th-century granite altarpieces and a charming 12th-century statue of the Virgin Mary (Notre-Dame-des-Marais) suckling a Child who looks well past weaning age.

Visit the castle (➤ 40–41) next, but take a walk outside the walls for an impressive overview before going inside. Walk the ramparts.

Notice the foundations of the keep (destroyed in 1166), and the waterwheels by the gatehouse.

Return to the upper town via rue de la Pinterie, a steep climb. More gardens halfway up the hill offer a chance to catch your breath, and a final panorama of the castle and river.

Distance 3km/2 miles (very hilly! – a little train will spare your legs if you can't face the final climb)
Time Allow half a day with time to look round the sights
Start/end point The tourist office in the upper town (2 rue Nationale) ✚ 16D
Lunch Crêperie Tivabro (€) ✉ 13 place du Marchix, 02 99 17 20 90

HÉDÉ

Woods and water are the lasting impressions of this hill village. Streams, cascades and ponds gleam all around, and lush, terraced gardens almost hide the crumbling stone houses and castle ruins perched on an outcrop of rock. In the churchyard, bronze memorials commemorate fallen war heroes.

Just north of the village at La Madeleine, the Ille-et-Rance canal passes through a magnificent staircase of 11 locks. The towpath walk is pleasant, though overgrown in places. A small exhibition about the Ille-et-Rance canal stands near the locks.

✚ 13D 🍴 Charming restaurants in quaint buildings, such as La Vieille Auberge, Hostellerie du Vieux Moulin, Le Genty Home (all on Tinténiac road, €€) 🚌 Line 8 (Rennes–St-Malo)
ℹ️ La Mairie, 02 99 45 46 18

MENHIR DE CHAMP-DOLENT

Just southeast of Dol-de-Bretagne, off the D795, is a large, single standing stone about 9m (30ft) high, stuck incongruously in a maize field. The menhir is alleged to have fallen from heaven to divide the armies of two warring brothers (Champ Dolent means 'Field of Sorrow'). It is said to be gradually sinking into the ground a couple of centimetres every century, and when it vanishes the world will end. The stone is freely accessible near the road, and can even be admired from a picnic table, though it has no markings or particular features of interest.
✚ 14C

REDON

This attractive flower-filled town is an important junction: roads, railways, waterways and regional boundaries converge here. The Nantes–Brest canal crosses the Vilaine at this point, joining the Oust to the north of the town. Ille-et-Vilaine, Morbihan and Loire-Atlantique meet on Redon's doorstep, and six major roads intersect. When the River Vilaine was fully navigable, Redon was a significant inland port. The elegant homes of former shipowners line the waterfront and parts of the old town. Today, river access to the south coast is blocked by the Arzal dam near La Roche-Bernard, but pleasure craft ply the local waterways in great numbers, negotiating Redon via a complicated series of locks.

The Grande Rue is one of its finest streets, full of splendid stone and half-timbered buildings decked with bright window-boxes.

Redon's main landmark is the church of St-Sauveur, a curious mixture of styles. A Romanesque lantern tower sits unexpectedly on Gothic buttressing, with a separate bell tower near by. The **Musée de la Batellerie** charts the history of the port and its waterborne trade. Redon makes an enjoyable excursion base for a day or two, with useful hotels and some excellent restaurants. You can hire bikes, canoes or canal boats from numerous outlets in the town and port. In late autumn, the chestnut forests on the outskirts of town take centre stage in a festival called the Fête de Teillouse. During the October harvest, local restaurants compete to produce chestnut-based dishes – its terrines are justly renowned.

The quiet moorland around St-Just, about 18km (11 miles) northeast of Redon, is sprinkled with neolithic monuments. The standing stones and dolmens at Landes de Cojoux and Croix St-Pierre can be freely explored (summer weekend guided tours, French only, from St-Just).

www.tourisme-pays-redon.com

✚ 24H 🍴 Good choice in town centre and port, such as La Bogue, 3 rue des États (€€) 🚌 10 (La Gacilly–Rochefort-en-Terre), 10B (Rennes) 🚆 Rennes, Vannes, Quimper and Nantes ⛴ River and canal cruises along the Oust and down the Vilaine to the Arzal dam; boat hire ❓ Fête de Teillouse (a chestnut festival and gastronomic fair, late Oct) 🛈 Place de la République, 02 99 71 06 04

Musée de la Batellerie

✉ Quai Jean-Bart ☎ 02 99 72 30 95 🕐 15 Jun–15 Sep daily 10–12, 3–6; Mon, Wed and weekends 2–6 off-peak ✋ Inexpensive

RENNES

Rennes is a burgeoning industrial and academic centre with a cosmopolitan air. Its inland location entices few holidaymakers from the coastal areas, but it's worth a day's excursion. Driving and parking in the city centre can be difficult, but Rennes is well served by public transport from most Breton cities. The central sights are compact and easily explored on foot. Nightlife is lively, especially in the old quarter. During July, Rennes hosts a major arts festival called Les Tombées de la Nuit (www.ville-rennes.fr), where rock and jazz fans congregate.

The city developed in Roman times from a

Gaulish settlement. It became a strategic route-hub, the Breton capital in 1562, and played a leading role in Brittany's struggle to retain an independent voice after unification with France. In 1720, a fire in the old town burned for nearly a week. The charred centre was rebuilt in neoclassical style. Today, examples of this grand civic architecture stand alongside the medieval buildings that survived the fire. In 1994 the Palais du Parlement (Breton Parliament) was badly damaged during fish-price riots. It has now been restored to its former glory. The Hôtel de Ville (town hall) dominates the place de la Marie. St-Pierre, Rennes' cathedral, is a relatively undistinguished 19th-century building containing a fine Flemish altarpiece. East of the old town, the peaceful Jardin

du Thabor was once the garden of the Benedictine abbey of St-Melaine.

Rennes has several excellent museums. The **Musée des Beaux-Arts** has an important collection. The **Musée de Bretagne** has been relocated at Les Champs Libres, a dynamic cultural centre with an interactive science museum, planetarium and exhibition galleries. Southeast, at Ferme de la Bintinais, the **Ecomusée du Pays de Rennes** traces the evolution of agricultural life in Brittany from the 16th century.

www.tourisme-rennes.com

🚏 14E 🍴 Le Café Breton (€), 14 rue Nantaise, 02 99 30 74 95 🚇 The Métro is mainly geared to commuter travel (www.star.fr) 🚌 Major route hub for inter-urban and local services; many local buses 🚆 National TGV and regional services throughout Brittany ✈ International and domestic flights (Air France/Ryanair/Flybe)

ℹ 11 rue St-Yves, 02 99 67 11 11

Musée des Beaux-Arts

🚩 *Rennes 3c* ✉ 20 quai Émile Zola ☎ 02 23 62 17 45; www.mbar.org 🕐 Wed–Sun 10–12, 2–6, Tue 10–6. Closed Mon and public hols 💶 Moderate 🚇 République

Musée de Bretagne

🚩 *Rennes 4e* ✉ 10 cours des Allies ☎ 02 23 40 66 70; www.leschampslibres.fr 🕐 Tue 12–9, Wed–Fri 12–7, Sat, Sun 2–7 💶 Moderate

Ecomusée du Pays de Rennes

🚩 *Rennes 3f (off map)* ✉ South of centre on Noyal–Chatillon road ☎ 02 99 51 38 15; www.ecomusee-rennes-metropole.fr 🕐 Apr–Sep Tue–Fri 9–6; Oct–Mar 9–12, 2–6, Sat 2–6, Sun 2–7; closed Mon and public hols 💶 Moderate 🚌 Line 61 🚆 Triangle

a walk around old Rennes

Start in place de la Mairie by the imposing Hôtel de Ville.

This building with its huge clock tower is one of Jacques Gabriel's most confident municipal statements after the great fire of 1720 (free guided tours in July and August). Opposite stands a charmingly ornate theatre.

Head west along rue du Guesclin, then north along rue Clisson and west again along rue de la Monnaie.

Notice the rococo-style church of St-Sauveur. Our Lady of Miracles saved Rennes from the English in 1357. Marble plaques thank her for latterday favours, including success in exams. The cathedral of St-Pierre, a 19th-century building in Roman style, contains a Flemish altarpiece in a side chapel. Find the light-switch to enjoy its amazing 3-D effects.

Thread through a quaint maze of streets lined with picturesque houses south of the cathedral, then north via rue des Dames.

The Porte-Mordelaise is the last remnant of the 15th-century ramparts, through which the dukes of Brittany passed for their coronations.

Head northeast through place des Lices.

Medieval jousts were held in this fine old square. The art nouveau *halles* (covered market) dates from 1622.

Pass through place St-Michel and place Ste-Anne, head south via place du Champ Jacquet, then east along rue la Fayette and rue Nationale to place du Parlement de Bretagne.

The tall, stripy buildings in place du Champ Jacquet are 17th-century, predating the Great Fire. Brittany's restored Parliament building makes an impressive statement on a spacious square of orderly gardens.

Head east along rue Victor Hugo, north up rue du Général M Guillaudot and through the Jardin du Thabor via place St-Mélaine. Finish the walk on the south bank of the river, at the Musée des Beaux-Arts (quai Émile Zola).

Distance 3.5km (2 miles)
Time Half a day, including visiting the main sights
Start point Hôtel de Ville ✚ *Rennes 2c*
End point Musée des Beaux-Arts ✚ *Rennes 3c*
Lunch Lots of choice en route. Try Crêperie Ste-Anne (€), 5 place Ste-Anne, 02 99 79 22 72

LA ROCHE AUX FÉES

Stranded way inland some 15km (9 miles) west of La Guerche-de-Bretagne, La Roche aux Fées attracts far fewer visitors than Carnac or Locmariaquer. It is, however, a most impressive megalithic monument, consisting of 42 slabs of mauve schist carefully balanced into what looks like an *allée couverte* or gallery grave high enough to walk upright inside (freely accessible). There is much speculation about its age and origins. Traditionally, engaged couples come here and separately count the stones. If they agree on the number, a happy future is presaged.

✚ 27G

ST-MALO
Best places to see, pages 54–55.

USINE MARÉMOTRICE DE LA RANCE
A huge concrete barrage blocks the mouth of the Rance, creating a large reservoir upstream, and used as a bridge by the St-Malo–Dinard road. From parking places at either end, walkways lead across the dam, from which you can watch sinewy torrents racing through the sluice gates with colossal force to the generators beneath. A visitor centre on the Dinard side explains its internal workings.

The dam was first opened in 1967, and spans 750m (820yds), curbing a reservoir of 22sq km (8.5sq miles). A lock surmounted by a swing-bridge enables sizeable boats to pass through. The 24 generators housed in a vast tunnel within the barrage generate over 600 million kWh a year, using both ebb and flow tides. However, this massively imaginative and costly project generates only about 3 per cent of Brittany's total electricity needs, and although it sounds environmentally friendly, its effects on local wildlife are significant.

www.edf.fr

✚ 13C ✉ La Richardais ☎ 02 99 16 37 14 🕐 Telephone for details of opening times ♿ Free 🚌 Lines 14 (St-Malo–Dinard), 11 (Dinan–Dinard) ⛴ Rance cruises; ferry (St-Malo–Dinard)

an excursion to Le Mont-St-Michel

The fickle course of the River Couesnant (the Norman boundary) now deprives Brittany by a hair's breadth of one of France's most evocative sights. The abbey-crowned island of Le Mont-St-Michel tapers mirage-like above the swirling mudflats of the bay. A golden statue of the Archangel Michael is poised on its topmost spire. It attracts more visitors than anywhere else in provincial France. Once in a lifetime, at least, everyone should see it. Arrive early to beat the crowds (preferably before 9am when the abbey opens).

Drive across the causeway, and park beside it, taking careful note of the tide tables (parts of the car park flood at high tide). Enter the island near the tourist office, and collect a plan of the site. Make your way up the steep, narrow Grande Rue, lined with souvenir shops and cafes.

The touristy village at the base of the Mount may be off-putting, but the medieval buildings are undeniably quaint. Soon the crowds thin out and the atmosphere becomes much more peaceful. Flights of steps lead everywhere, and it's a steep climb. Several little museums can be visited on the way to the abbey. The Musée Maritime is an exhibition about the bay and its exceptional tides, which race across the flat sands faster than a horse can gallop (or so it is claimed). Next is the Archéoscope, an archangelic multimedia presentation about the abbey (St Michael is your guide). Still further up near the parish church is Tiphaine's House, built by the medieval warrior Bertrand Du Guesclin (then commander of the Mount) for his scholarly wife in 1365.

Continue up the hill and enter the abbey.

The abbey is a masterpiece of Romanesque and Gothic architecture. Founded in 708 by the Bishop of Avranches, it has been a place of pilgrimage for over a thousand years. Known as La Merveille (The Marvel), it seems as delicately balanced as a house of cards, some sections cantilevered over thin air, others tightly buttressed to the living granite. Beyond the church, a signed route leads through the refectory, cloisters and Knights' Hall to the crypt.

After visiting the interior, take a walk around the ramparts and gardens for a breathtaking overview of the abbey and the bay.

Distance 1km (half a mile)

Time Allow half a day to see the main sights

Start/end point Tourist office ✠ 15C
🚌 Line 17 (St-Malo–Pontorson), then Line 6, or some direct services from St-Malo (Les Courriers Breton)

Lunch A choice of cafes and restaurants in the village, such as La Mère Poulard (€–€€€), Grande Rue, 02 33 89 68 68 or Les Terrasses Poulard (€€), 02 33 89 02 02

Abbey

☎ 02 33 89 80 00;
www.ot-montsaintmichel.com or
www.monum.fr

🕐 May–Aug daily 9–7; Sep–Apr 9:30–6 (abbey church service Tue–Sat 12:15, Sun 11:30)

✋ No charge to visit the Mount, but parking and sights expensive. Abbey ticket price includes a choice of self-guided, escorted or audio-tours; individual or combined tickets are available for the museums

VITRÉ

After Dinan, Vitré is perhaps Brittany's best-preserved medieval town. Close to the town, a hilly belvedere by the Vilaine, called the Tertres Noires, gives a splendid view of its bristling turrets, drum towers and ramparts. The **château** dates mainly from the 13th century, but was enlarged and modified during the 16th and restored after years of neglect in the late 19th century. Vitré's location on the borders between France and Brittany made it a constant target during struggles in the Middle Ages. The castle houses several interesting **museums.**

The old town stretches through cobbled hilly streets below the castle. Some if its half-timbered houses are now converted into shops and restaurants. Best are those along rue de la Baudrairie. Much of the town's revenue comes from tourism; in former centuries its prosperity came mostly from the textile trade. Wealthy merchants settled here and built fine mansions.

Southeast of Vitré stands Madame de Sevigné's former home, the Château des Rochers-Sevigné.

www.ot-vitre.fr

✚ 15E 🍴 Le Potagér (€–€€), place du Général Leclerc, 02 99 74 68 88
🚌 Line 14 (Fougères), 20 (La Guerche-de-Bretagne) 🚆 Rennes, Normandy
🛈 Place du Général-de-Gaulle, 02 99 75 04 46

Château/museums

✉ Place du Château ☎ 02 99 75 04 54 🕐 May–Sep Wed–Mon 10–12:45, 2–6; Oct–Apr Mon, Wed–Sat 10–12:15, 2–5:30, Sun 2–5:30 ✋ Inexpensive (museum pass for entrance to all museums and Château des Rochers-Sevigné)

HOTELS

CANCALE
Continental (€€–€€€)
Watch the bobbing boats from this attractive waterfront hotel. The excellent restaurant dishes up the likes of turbot in a salt crust and salt marsh lamb.

✉ 4 quai Thomas ☎ 02 99 89 60 16; www.hotel-cancale.com
🕐 Closed mid-Jan to mid-Feb

Le Chatellier (€)
Lovely, quiet stone house about a mile from Cancale. Rooms, some of which overlook the garden, are stylishly decorated in shades of grey and beige with *Toile de Jouy* bedspreads.

✉ Route de St-Malo ☎ 02 99 89 81 84; www.hotellechatellier.com
🕐 Closed Dec–Jan

CHÂTEAUBOURG
Pen-Roc (€€–€€€)
A bright, luxurious hotel in a modernized farmhouse with rural surroundings and lovely grounds. Excellent facilities and ambitious cooking. Golf and spa packages available.

✉ La Peinière, St-Didier ☎ 02 99 00 33 02; www.penroc.fr
🕐 Closed mid-Dec to mid-Jan

COMBOURG
Du Château (€–€€€)
A comfortable hotel with some rooms overlook the castle. Shady terrace for summer dining and a generous buffet breakfast.

✉ 1 place Chateaubriand ☎ 02 99 73 00 38; www.hotelduchateau.com
🕐 Closed mid-Dec to mid-Jan; Sun eve Oct–Mar

DINARD
Hotel de la Plage (€–€€)
Sea views and dark wood are notable features of this traditional stone villa. Savour breakfast on the terrace overlooking the beach.

✉ 3 boulevard Féart ☎ 02 99 46 14 87; www.hoteldelaplage-dinard.com
🕐 Closed Jan

Reine Hortense (€€€)

Refined *fin-de-siècle* villa with sweeping views over the beach. Expect antiques, paintings and a silver-plated bath.

✉ 19 rue Malouine ☎ 02 99 46 54 31; www.villa-reine-hortense.com
🕐 Closed Oct–Mar

FOUGÈRES
La Lanterne (€)

Bed-and-breakfast in an attractive 17th-century house near the castle. A simple, value-for-money base for exploring.

✉ 110 rue de la Pinterie ☎ 02 99 99 58 80

LA GOUESNIÈRE
Tirel-Guérin (€–€€€)

Acclaimed restaurant-with-rooms beside a quaint old railway station near Cancale. Excellent facilities include an indoor swimming pool and fitness centre. Gourmet cooking.

✉ Gare de la Gouesnière, St-Méloir-des-Ondes ☎ 02 99 89 10 46; www.tirel-guerin.com 🕐 Closed mid-Dec to Jan

RENNES
Le Coq-Gadby (€€–€€€)

In a quiet residential district, this eco-friendly hotel and spa in spacious grounds has the air of an elegant private home, with antiques and *objets d'art*. Acclaimed restaurant.

✉ 156 rue d'Antrain ☎ 02 99 38 05 55; www.lecoq-gadby.com

Hotel de Nemours (€–€€)

Stylish boutique hotel in the city centre. Rooms are decorated in neutral shades and photos of old Rennes adorn the corridors.

✉ 5 rue de Nemours ☎ 02 99 78 26 26; www.hotelnemours.com

ST-MALO
Le Beaufort (€€–€€€)

Chic decor in cool muted tones gives this seafront hotel a classy feel. Relax with an aperitif in the piano bar.

✉ 25 chaussée de Sillon ☎ 02 99 40 99 99; www.hotel-beaufort.com

Le Nautilus (€)

Cosy, warm-toned rooms in a listed building in the heart of St-Malo, where breakfast is simple but delicious. Ask the friendly staff what to see and do in the area.

✉ 9 rue de la Corne de Serf ☎ 02 99 40 42 27; www.lenautilus.com
🕐 Closed mid-Nov to mid-Dec, Jan

La Rance (€–€€)

This friendly and civilized little place at Port Solidor has lovely estuary views and well-equipped, traditionally furnished bedrooms which have recently been redecorated. As well as a choice of restaurants nearby, you're close to the ferry terminal.

✉ 15 quai Sébastopol, St-Servan ☎ 02 99 81 78 63; www.larancehotel.com
🕐 Closed Nov to mid-Jan

San Pedro (€)

The rooms are bright and simple but the welcome is warm in this nautical-themed hotel. Guests love the daily breakfast specials: *far breton* on Wednesday, *crêpes* on Friday.

✉ 1 rue St-Anne ☎ 02 9940 88 57; www.sanpedro-hotel.com 🕐 Closed mid-Nov to Mar

ST-SULIAC
Les Mouettes (€)

Bright, flowery rooms on the main street of one of France's prettiest villages. Try the owner's home-made jams for breakfast before heading off to explore the Rance river.

✉ 17 Grande Rue ☎ 02 99 58 30 41; www.les-mouettes-saint-suliac.com

LE TRONCHET
Le Mesnil des Bois (€€)

An elegant bed-and-breakfast between Dinan and Dol in a characterful 16th-century manor surrounded by parkland. Nibble a breakfast croissant by the wood fire in winter; play board games on rainy days.

✉ Le Tronchet ☎ 02 99 58 97 12; www.le-mesnil-des-bois.com
🕐 Closed Nov–Feb

RESTAURANTS

CANCALE
Le Cancalais (€–€€)
One of the best waterfront restaurants in La Houle. You're assured of a warm welcome in the bright, rustic dining room where most people are tucking into a seafood platter.

✉ Quai Gambetta ☎ 02 99 89 61 93; www.lecancalais.com ⏰ Daily 12–2, 7–9; closed Jan, Sun eve, Mon

DINARD
Didier Méril (€€)
Polished, affable service and accomplished cooking in sleek, modern premises near the beach and casino. The regularly changing menus include roast turbot drizzled with pistachio oil.

✉ 1 place Général de Gaulle ☎ 02 99 46 95 74 ⏰ Daily 12:15–2:30, 7:15–9:30; closed late Nov–early Dec

FOUGÈRES
Crêperie Tivabro (€)
You'll find some of the best pancakes in Brittany in this pretty stone cottage. Try *La Folliard* – banana drenched in salted-butter caramel topped with *tarte tatin* ice cream.

✉ 13 place du Marchix ☎ 02 99 17 20 90 ⏰ Tue–Sun 12–2, 7–9; closed Mon, Wed eve and Sun eve (except Jul, Aug)

Les Voyageurs (€–€€)
Reliable, classic cooking in the upper town. You'll find grilled pork chops and lobster fricassee on the menu.

✉ 10 place Gambetta ☎ 02 99 99 14 17 ⏰ Daily 12–2, 7:30–9:30; closed Fri, Sat lunch Oct–Apr

LA GUERCHE-DE-BRETAGNE
La Calèche (€–€€)
Good-value lunch menus in a bright dining room near La Roche aux Fées. Pork belly infused with rosemary hits the spot.

✉ 16 avenue Général Leclerc ☎ 02 99 96 21 63 ⏰ Daily 12:30–1:30, 7:30–9; closed early Aug, Christmas, New Year, Mon, Fri eve, Sun eve

HÉDÉ
La Vieille Auberge (€–€€€)
A pretty, terraced restaurant in a 17th-century granite house beside a lake. Seasonal menus include crab and salmon gazpacho.

✉ Route de Tinténiac ☎ 02 99 45 46 25 🕐 Daily 12:15–1:15, 7:30–9:15; closed late Aug–early Sep, mid-Feb to early Mar, Sun eve, Mon

REDON
La Bogue (€€)
Enterprising regional cooking in a quaint setting near the town hall. Seasonal chestnut specialities.

✉ 3 rue des Etats ☎ 02 99 71 12 95 🕐 Daily 12:15–1:15, 7:15–9; closed Sun eve, Mon

RENNES
Au Marché des Lices (€)
A fine *crêperie* in the marketplace, with a cosy, rustic interior. No formal menus, but tasty *plats du jour* as well as pancakes.

✉ 3 place du Bas des Lices ☎ 02 99 30 42 95 🕐 Mon–Sat 12–2, 7–9; closed early Jan, 3 weeks Aug, Sun

Le Galopin (€–€€€)
Smart, traditional wood-fronted brasserie. The menu features lamb chops with fennel seeds and vegetable ratatouille.

✉ 21 avenue Janvier ☎ 02 99 31 55 96 🕐 Daily 12–2, 7–11pm; closed Aug, Sat lunch and Sun

ST-MALO
À la Duchesse Anne (€€€)
A long-established restaurant built into the ramparts. Specialities include lobster and *tarte tatin*. Reserve ahead.

✉ 5 place Guy La Chambre ☎ 02 99 40 85 33 🕐 Daily 12:15–1:30, 7:15–9:30; closed Dec–Jan, Mon lunch, Wed, Sun eve Oct–Apr

Le Brigantine (€)
This popular old-town *crêperie* in a stone building has a keen following for omelettes, pancakes and inexpensive light meals. Try

a *galette* filled with *soubise* – onions pickled in cider.
✉ 13 rue de Dinan ☎ 02 99 56 82 82 ⏱ Daily 12–10pm; closed late Nov, most of Jan, Tue, Wed (except school hols)

ST-MÉLOIR-DES-ONDES
Le Coquillage (€€–€€€)
Sophisticated seafood in a 1920s waterfront villa owned by celebrated chef Olivier Roellinger. Sea bream *tartare* with vegetables stewed in butter, seaweed and ginger sets the tone.
✉ Château Richeux, D155 Route de Mont-St-Michel ☎ 02 99 89 64 76; www.maisons-de-bricourt.com ⏱ Daily 12–1:30, 7:30–9:30; closed mid-Jan to Feb

VITRÉ
Le Potager (€–€€)
Aubergine and orange tones on the walls and the likes of duck breast with honey and lime on the table make this bistro a pleasant lunch stop. Good-value set menus.
✉ 5 place Général Leclerc ☎ 02 99 74 68 88 ⏱ Daily 12–1:30, 7:30–9:30; closed 2 weeks Aug, Sat lunch, Sun eve and Mon

SHOPPING

CRAFTS
St-Méloir-des-Ondes, between Cancale and Dol-de-Bretagne, is a well-known crafts centre. In summer a number of artisans' workshops and studios can be visited.

L'Atelier du Verre
Watch skilled craftsmen blow glass into a kaleidoscopic range of bright decorative objects. On-site showrooms.
✉ 4 rue de Radegonde, St-Méloir-des-Ondes ☎ 02 99 89 18 10; www.idverre.net/durand-gasselin ⏱ Daily 10–12:30, 2:30–6:30; pm only Sun, Mon

Ateliers Helmbold
A specialist glassworks southeast of Rennes, producing decorative housewares and imaginative contemporary works (mirrors, vases, stained-glass panels etc).

✉ Le Choizel, Corps-Nuds ☎ 02 99 44 12 37; www.ateliers-helmbold.com
🕐 Mon–Fri 8–12, 1:30–5:30

La Droguerie de Marine

A marine chandler selling ship's models, compasses and regional products. Some English-language books.
✉ 66 rue Georges Clemenceau, St-Servan ☎ 02 99 81 60 39 🕐 Mon 2–7, Tue–Sat 10–12:30, 2:30–7; closed Sun

FOOD AND DRINK
Le Chèvrerie du Désert

A goat farm selling home-made cheese and other regional foods.
✉ Le Désert, Plerguer ☎ 02 99 58 92 14 🕐 Jul, Aug daily 11–6:30; Apr–Jun, Aug–Sep Wed–Mon 2:30–6:30

Chocolaterie Durand

A lovely 19th-century building selling chocolate in unusual flavours. Addictive caramel spreads flavoured with whisky, ginger etc.
✉ 5 quai Chateaubriand, Rennes ☎ 02 99 78 10 00 🕐 Thu–Mon 10–12:30, 2:30–6:30; closed Tue, Wed

Grain de Vanille

Top chef Olivier Roellinger's tiny, unobtrusive master-bakery selling biscuits, cakes, speciality bread, home-made ice cream, buckwheat flakes and more. On-site *salon de thé*.
✉ 12 place de la Victoire, Cancale ☎ 02 23 15 12 70;
www.maisons-de-bricourt.com

ENTERTAINMENT

Casino Barrière de Dinard

Excusive casino overlooking Dinard's superb main beach. Dinner shows, live music, cocktail bar. Food served all day. Smart dress.
✉ 4 boulevard Wilson, Dinard ☎ 02 99 16 30 30; www.lucienbarriere.com
🕐 Gaming tables: daily Jul, Aug; Wed–Fri from 9pm, Sat–Sun until 4am

Cine Manivel

Avant-garde cinema next to the maritime museum putting on

independent art-house films, some in *version originale* (vo after the title). There's a foyer cafe with occasional live music.

✉ 12 quai Jean Bart, Redon ☎ 02 99 72 28 20; www.cinemanivel.fr

Le Coquelicot

On a hilly street near the old town, this popular bar is a well-known pub-concert offering live music (jazz, folk, rock, blues etc) and cafe-theatre. Some 70 different beers are on sale.

✉ 18 rue de Vitré, Fougères ☎ 02 99 99 84 52; www.barcoquelicot.free.fr
🕐 Tue–Sat 3pm–1am

Le Cunningham

A lively bar down by the yacht harbour in St-Servan, beautifully panelled in chestnut wood by a ship's carpenter. Live music all year – jazz soirées, Latin, soul.

✉ 2 rue des Hauts-Sablons, St-Servan, St-Malo ☎ 02 99 81 48 08; www.st-malo-hotel-cunningham.com 🕐 Tue–Sun from 6pm

Péniche Spectacle

Two barges make unusual venues for world music, jazz, cabaret, workshops, readings and exhibitions. Performances for children. Phone to reserve tickets.

✉ 30 quai St-Cyr, Rennes ☎ 02 99 59 35 38; www.penichespectacle.com
🕐 Shows normally Thu–Sat

Théâtre National de Bretagne (TNB)

A leading arts venue with three separate performance halls for drama, dance, jazz and classical music. Also cinema screenings of independent films in their original language. Restaurant and bar.

✉ 1 rue St-Hélier, Rennes ☎ 02 99 31 12 31; www.t-n-b.fr 🕐 Box office: Tue–Fri 1–7, Sat 2–7

Théâtre St-Malo

This leading theatre hosts major touring productions, concerts, opera, big band, plays, musicals and children's performances.

✉ 6 place Bouvet, St-Malo ☎ 02 99 81 62 61; www.theatresaintmalo.com
🕐 Box office: Tue–Fri 10–12, 2–6:30, Sat 10–12, 2–6

Loire-Atlantique

In 1973, Brittany's southeastern wing was torn away to form part of a neighbouring region, Pays-de-la-Loire. But for many Bretons, the natural boundary of Brittany is still the final reach of the River Loire. In this book, Loire-Atlantique is treated as part of Brittany, at least as far as that great southern moat.

Nantes

The beaches are among Brittany's best. Besides the magnificent crescent of sand at La Baule, or Monsieur Hulot's holiday beach at St-Marc, there are many unspoilt hideaways. Nature-lovers will enjoy the fascinating boglands of La Grande Brière, now a regional park, and the strange saltmarshes of Guérande.

Inland, Loire-Atlantique has fine border castles at Ancenis, Châteaubriant and Grand-Fougeray. The waterways around Nantes and the canals of La Grande Brière suggest interesting boat trips. Highlight of this *département*, though, is Nantes, Brittany's former capital and one of France's liveliest provincial centres.

BATZ-SUR-MER

At Batz, the low-lying salt marshes are interrupted by the 60m (197ft) pepperpot tower of St-Guénolé, a prominent land- and seamark (climbable – excellent views). The chancel is draped with fishing nets, a reminder of its seafaring patronage. The ruined chapel behind St-Guénolé is Notre-Dame-du-Mûrier (Our Lady of the Mulberry Tree), legendarily built by a 15th-century nobleman saved from shipwreck by the light of a miraculous burning tree. In rue Pasteur is the **Musée des Marais Salants** (Saltmarsh Museum), a fascinating exhibition about the local salt industry. On the coast road to Le Pouliguen, **Le Grand Blockhaus** recreates life in a World War II German command post in one of the biggest concrete bunkers of the Atlantic Wall.

www.marie-batzsurmer.fr

✚ 22K 🚌 Lines E or L (Le Croisic–La Baule)

🛈 25 rue de la Plage, 02 40 23 92 36

Musée des Marais Salants
✉ 29 bis rue Pasteur ☎ 02 40 23 82 79; www.maraissalants.com
🕐 Jul–Sep daily 10–12, 2:30–7; Jun 10–12, 2–6; Oct–May times vary
✋ Inexpensive

Le Grand Blockhaus
✉ Côte Sauvage ☎ 02 40 23 88 29; www.grand-blockhaus.com
🕐 Apr to mid-Nov and Feb hols daily 10–7 ✋ Moderate

LA BAULE

La Baule-Escoublac is one of the smartest and largest resorts in northern France, packed at weekends with affluent sophisticates from Paris and other cities. The low-lying seafront, periodically engulfed in Loire silt and shifting sands, supported a single fishing village, Escoublac, until 1840, when pine trees were planted to stabilize the dunes and act as a windbreak. In 1879, after the arrival of the railway, the first holiday developments began to appear.

A 5km (3-mile) beach of gleaming golden sand is its main attraction, shelving so gently that you can safely wade far out to sea. Apartment blocks and hotels line the seafront road, some awesomely grand, most charmlessly modern and boxlike. Behind lie tree-lined avenues of villas dating from a more gracious belle époque age. The marina at Le Pouliguen is full of elegant craft.

La Baule offers every kind of seaside diversion, from genteel pursuits like bridge and golf to a casino and the latest high-tech watersports and thalassotherapy. The streets near place de la Victoire bristle with upmarket shops and restaurants, and during the season the social diary is never empty.

✚ 23K 🍴 Nossy Bé (€–€€), at the beach, 02 40 60 42 25 🚌 Lines A, D, E, G, H, J, N (Guérande, Pénestin, St-Nazaire. *Petit train* (tourist train) along seafront to Pornichet 🚉 Regular TGV connections with Paris
ℹ 8 place de la Victoire, 02 40 24 34 44; www.labaule.fr

CHÂTEAUBRIANT

Set well inland amid lake-strewn woodland, Châteaubriant stands guard on the Anjou border, part of the line of fortified bastions protecting Brittany from invasion. Its red sandstone church, St-Jean-de-Béré, dates back to the 11th century; its altarpieces are mostly 17th century. The main landmark is the **castle,** a piecemeal structure, partly feudal, partly Renaissance. The keep is the oldest section; the Seigneurial Palace was built by Jean de Laval, Count of Châteaubriant. A balcony at the top of the central staircase overlooks the Court of Honour gardens and the rest of the castle.

www.tourisme-chateaubriant.fr

🚌 27H 🍴 Restaurants on outskirts; simple eating places near castle, such as Le Bilig (€), place St-Nicolas, 02 40 81 48 49 🚌 Lines 40, 41, 42, 44 (Angers, Nantes, St-Nazaire) 🚆 Rennes and Nantes

🛈 22 rue de Couéré ☎ 02 40 28 20 90

Château de Châteaubriant

✉ Rue du Château ☎ 02 40 28 20 90 🕐 May–Sep Wed–Mon 11–6:30, Oct–Apr 2–5:30. Guided tours May–Sep Wed–Mon (Sat–Sun only off season) ✋ Inexpensive

LE CROISIC

Le Croisic occupies a bulbous headland on the shores of the Grand Traict lagoon. Three islets linked by bridges form separate basins in the port, a picturesque scene when the fishing fleets arrive with catches of prawn. A modern *criée* (fish market) occupies one of these islands. You can watch the early-morning proceedings from a gallery (5am). The pleasantly shabby old town near by contains 17th-century houses with wrought-iron balconies. Port-Lin, on the bracing ocean side of Le Croisic, is the main resort area, where several hotels overlook the waves crashing on dark rocks. Le Croisic's main attraction is its splendid **Océarium,** a star-shaped aquarium with well-organized displays of local and exotic species. The fish-farming exhibits are particularly interesting: baby eels and fingernail-sized turbot gulp gently at their spectators, and mussels cluster like maritime grapes on wooden posts *(bouchots)*. The shark tank has a slightly alarming 'walk-through' tunnel.

www.ot-lecroisic.com

🚇 22K 🍴 Le St-Alys (€–€€), 3 quai Hervé Rielle, 02 40 23 58 40 🚌 Lines E, K (La Baule, St-Nazaire) 🚆 La Baule, Nantes, Paris (TGV), St-Nazaire
ℹ️ Place du 18 Juin 1940, 02 40 23 00 70

Océarium

✉️ Avenue de St-Goustan ☎️ 02 40 23 02 44; www.ocearium-croisic.fr
🕐 Apr–Aug daily 10–6 (7 Jul, Aug); Nov, Dec 2–6; rest of year 12–12, 2–6; closed Jan ♿ Expensive 🍴 Snack-bar (€) ❓ Fish hand fed by scuba-diver

ici on reçoit
à pied à cheva
en voit

LA GRANDE BRIÈRE

Before the last ice age, the low-lying basin north of La Baule was covered with woodland. When the ice melted and sea levels rose, the area flooded and a thick layer of peat was formed. Gradually the sea retreated, and the marshes were drained and settled. The native Brièrons developed an insular lifestyle based on hunting, fishing and turf-cutting. Using local reeds to thatch their cottages and make wicker fish traps, they negotiated the marshes in flat-bottomed punts.

In 1970, the Grande Brière was designated a 20,000ha (49,420-acre) regional nature park. It is now a popular holiday area offering fishing, riding, birdwatching and boating. The main villages of Kerhinet, St-Lyphard and St-Joachim are clusters of tidily restored thatched cottages; several house restaurants, craft shops or little

ecomusées. Le Musée du Chaume (Thatch Museum), La Maison de l'Eclusier (Lock-Keeper's House) and La Maison de la Mariée (the Bride's House) are examples. La Réserve Ornithologique is a nature reserve with walks and hides (binocular hire).

www.parc-naturel-briere.fr

🕂 23K 🍴 Several auberges serve regional specialities, such as Le Nézil, St-Lyphard (€–€€; ➤ 165) 🚌 Lines C, D, G (Guérande–St-Lyphard) 🚣 Barge or punt *(chaland* or *blain)* hire or trips through the marshes

ℹ️ 38 rue de la Brière, La Chapelle-des-Marais, 02 40 66 85 01

GUÉRANDE

The medieval ramparts encircling Guérande are visible for miles across the flat *marais salants* (saltmarshes). Inside these tower-studded walls, the old town is a maze of quaint streets with overhanging timber-framed houses. The Porte St-Michel (the former governor's residence) contains an idiosyncratic local history museum.

South of Guérande, heaps of salt fringe a mosaic of glittering pools linked by sluice gates and drainage channels. Egrets and herons patrol the pans for fish. Seawater floods into the larger lagoons at high tide, trickling gradually into ever-smaller and shallower clay-lined pits *(oeillets)* to evaporate in the sun and wind. Purified salt is on sale by the roadside. Visit the nearby Maison des Paludiers (www.maisondespaludiers.fr) or the Terre de Sel (www.terredesel.fr), a lively interactive discovery centre on the salt industry.

www.ot-guerande.fr

🕂 23K 🍴 Good choice in old town, such as Roc-Maria (€; ➤ 165)

🚌 Lines A, B, D, G, H, J (St-Nazaire, La Baule, St-Lyphard/Grande Brière)

ℹ️ 1 place du Marché au Bois, 0 820 15 00 44

NANTES

Nantes' historic centre is full of good shops, restaurants and museums, most of it compact enough to explore on foot. It's a good base for visiting the vineyards and châteaux of the Loire Valley.

During the 16th to 18th centuries, the town prospered on the notorious 'ebony' (slave) trade with Africa and the Caribbean. As the Loire silted up, the port became inaccessible to large cargo vessels and Nantes diversified into other industries. Much of its attractive 18th- and 19th-century architecture remains intact despite war damage.

The **Château des Ducs de Bretagne** was built by François II (Duchess Anne's father) in 1466. It has been greatly altered throughout the centuries and now houses a museum devoted to the history of Nantes. Only the courtyard and ramparts can be visited free of charge. The **Musée Jules-Verne** has the largest collection of manuscripts, portraits and objects once belonging to the writer, born here in 1828. Near by in the upper town are the Cathédrale St-Pierre (➤ 38–39), and the **Musée des Beaux-Arts** (Fine Arts Museum), strong on 19th- and 20th-century art. The Jardin des Plantes contains an extensive collection of ancient magnolias and a huge Palmarium with a miniature jungle of exotic plants.

Towards the lower town are the 15th- and 16th-century houses of Ste-Croix and the shipowners' mansions in the Ancienne Île Feydeau. The **Palais Dobrée** has an excellent archaeological collection and many *objets d'art*, including a casket which once held the heart of Brittany's beloved Duchess Anne. The **Muséum d'Histoire Naturelle** is a fascinating 19th-century collection. Its most bizarre exhibit is the skin of a soldier whose dying wish was to be made into a drum.

www.nantes-tourisme.com

➕ 26L 🍴 La Cigale (€–€€€), 4 place Graslin, 02 51 84 94 94
🚌 Inner-city buses and trams (day pass) 🚆 Regional rail terminal; TGV connections with Paris 🚢 River cruises: Erdres, Loire, Sèvre
ℹ 3 rue Olivier de Clisson, 08 92 46 40 44

Château des Ducs de Bretagne

✉ 4 place Marc Elder ☎ 0 811 46 46 44; www.chateau-nantes.fr
🕐 Museum: Jul, Aug daily 9–7; Sep–Jun Tue–Sun 10–6.
Courtyard/ramparts: Jul, Aug daily 9–8; Sep–Jun 10–7
✋ Moderate

Musée Jules-Verne

✉ 3 rue de l'Hermitage ☎ 02 40 69 72 52;
www.nantes.fr/julesverne 🕐 Daily 10–12, 2–6; closed Tue and Sun am ✋ Inexpensive

Musée des Beaux-Arts

✉ 10 rue Clémenceau ☎ 02 51 17 45 00 🕐 Wed–Mon 10–6, Thu 10–8 ✋ Inexpensive

Palais Dobrée

✉ 18 rue Voltaire ☎ 02 40 71 03 50 🕐 Tue–Fri 1:30–5:30, Sat–Sun 2:30–5:30; closed Mon ✋ Inexpensive

Muséum d'Histoire Naturelle

✉ 12 rue Voltaire ☎ 02 40 41 55 00; www.museum.nantes.fr
🕐 Wed–Mon 10–6; closed Tue ✋ Inexpensive

a walk around old Nantes

Start in the place St-Pierre (by the cathedral).

After visiting the main sights (castle, cathedral and fine arts museum), relax for a while in the Jardin des Plantes.

Head back along rue de Richebourg, deviating briefly to the late Gothic Chapelle de l'Immaculée. Skirting the château, make for the Ste-Croix district via rue du Chât.

This is one of the oldest and most delightful parts of Nantes. Here 15th- and 16th-century houses line the streets (see rue de la Baclerie, rue de la Juiverie and rue du Bouffay near the church of Ste-Croix).

Walk down rue d'Orléans to place Royale.

Here the architecture leaps ahead a couple of hundred years to the 18th century. The central fountain represents the Loire and its tributaries. A block southwest, passage Pommeraye is an elegant *fin-de-siècle* shopping centre.

Take rue de la Pérouse from place Royale, then turn west into place du Commerce (the tourist office is here).

The Ancienne Île Feydeau to the southeast, once embraced by arms of the Loire, is no longer an island. It has many wealthy shipowners' houses decorated with quaint carvings and ornate wrought-ironwork.

Head up rue J J Rousseau into place Graslin.

This fine square has a mix of 18th- and 19th-century buildings, best appreciated from the tables outside the brasserie La Cigale (➤ 59). The art nouveau interior is

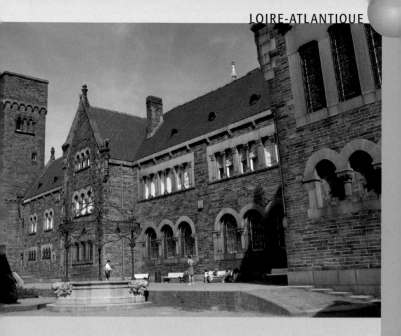

a riot of mirrors, mosaic tiles and swirling plasterwork.

Take cours Cambronne southwest of place Graslin, another fine collection of 18th- and 19th-century houses. Head for the waterfront (quai de la Fosse).

The Musée de l'Imprimerie (No 24) is an interesting little museum of printing, with working machinery.

Finish the walk at the Dobrée museum complex (➤ 159) on rue Voltaire.

Distance 4km (2.5 miles)
Time Allow most of the day if you want to see museums or do some shopping.
Start point Place St-Pierre 🚌 26L
End point Palais Dobrée 🚌 26L
Lunch La Cigale (€–€€€; ➤ 59)

ST-NAZAIRE

St-Nazaire was all but obliterated during World War II and most of the city was later rebuilt in rather brutal, functional concrete. Today, several of its high-profile visitor attractions reveal St-Nazaire's key role in France's maritime history.

The **Ecomusée** at the heart of the port traces the story of the town, with special emphasis on the wartime era. The best section is the submarine exit, a covered lock from which U-boats could slip out of the harbour in secret. It now contains the French nuclear-powered submarine *Espadon*, which once sailed the polar ice-caps (the museum ticket includes a tour of the vessel – living quarters, engines and torpedo room).

St-Nazaire's shipbuilding industry has declined sharply, but some vessels are still built here, including the huge cruise-liner *Queen Mary 2* in recent times. **Escal'Atlantic** is an impressive discovery centre recreating the world of the ocean liner, with multimedia special effects and historic movie footage. Other attractions in the port complex include the **Aker shipyards.** Out of town at Gron is the **French Airbus factory** (tours of both available; book ahead and take your passport).

South of the town a suspension bridge arcs across the Loire, providing a fast link from Brittany to the Atlantic seaboard.

www.saint-nazaire-tourisme.com

🚑 23K 🍴 Le Sabayon (€–€€), 7 rue de la Paix, 02 40 01 88 21 🚌 Lines to Guérande, La Baule, Pornichet, St-Marc 🚉 La Baule, Nantes, Paris 🚢 River cruises to Nantes: 02 40 69 40 40; www.marineetloire.fr

ℹ️ Base Sous-Marine, boulevard de la Légion d'Honneur, 02 40 22 40 65

Port museums and dockland attractions

✉️ Ville-Port ☎ 02 28 54 06 40; Aker shipyards: www.stxeurope.com; Ecomusée: www.ecomusee-saint-nazaire.com; Escal'Atlantic: http://escale-atlantic.com 🕐 Dates and times vary, call or check online for details 💰 Expensive

HOTELS

BATZ-SUR-MER
Le Lichen de la Mer (€€–€€€)
Traditional waterfront hotel with panoramic Côte Sauvage views
from some rooms. They also have a villa to rent.
✉ Baie du Manérick ☎ 02 40 23 91 92; www.le-lichen.com

LA BAULE
Castel Marie-Louise (€€€)
Exclusive hotel and acclaimed restaurant in a belle époque villa
shaded by pine trees. Borrow a bicycle (free) to explore the coast.
✉ 1 avenue Andrieu ☎ 02 40 11 48 38; www.castel-marie-louise.com
🕐 Closed Jan

Mona Lisa (€–€€)
Value-for-money boutique hotel near the station. Rooms have been
refurbished in contemporary style: the premium ones have
hydromassage showers, all have king-size beds. Nice pool.
✉ 42 avenue Georges Clemenceau ☎ 02 40 60 21 33;
www.hotelmonalisa-labaule.com.

BRIÈRE
La Mare aux Oiseaux (€€€)
A typical Brière thatched cottage with charming, stylish bedrooms.
Enjoy some creative regional cuisine from Eric Guéin.
✉ 162 Île de Fedrun ☎ 02 40 88 53 01; www.mareauxoiseaux.fr 🕐 Closed
Jan–Mar

LE CROISIC
Fort de l'Océan (€€€)
A sophisticated hideaway in a clifftop location attracting many
celebrities for its designer interior and fashionable restaurant.
✉ Pointe du Croisic ☎ 02 40 15 77 77; www.hotelfortocean.com

NANTES
Hotel St Yves (€)
This little hotel is well placed for the train station and sights.

Charming owners advise on what to see and are cyclist-friendly.

✉ 154 avenue du Général Buat ☎ 02 40 74 48 42; www.hotel-saintyves.fr

PORNICHET
Villa Flornoy (€–€€)

This refined villa has elegant bedrooms. The small well-kept garden is ideal for breakfast or a pre-dinner aperitif.

✉ 7 avenue Flornoy ☎ 02 40 11 60 00; www.villa-flornoy.com
🕐 Closed mid-Nov to Jan

PIRIAC-SUR-MER
Villa Brambell (€€)

Discerning guests will adore the two charming rooms in this artist-owned, 19th-century villa. There's direct access to the beach.

✉ 3 rue des Pétrels ☎ 02 40 23 50 21; www.villa-brambell.fr

RESTAURANTS

LA BAULE
La Ferme du Grand Clos (€–€€)

This smart farmhouse *crêperie* towards Le Pouliguen offers dishes like *cassoulet* and duck *confit* as well as delicious pancakes. Try *L'Eog* – five types of seaweed with smoked salmon.

✉ 52 avenue de Lattre-de-Tassigny ☎ 02 40 60 03 30 🕐 Daily 12–2, 7–10; closed mid-Nov to mid-Dec, Mon–Wed Oct–Mar

Nossy Bé (€–€€)

Fashionable beach-side bar-restaurant. Asian-fusion cuisine such as king prawns in lemon and ginger or sweet and sour tuna steak.

✉ Plage de la Baule ☎ 02 40 60 42 25; www.nossybe.com 🕐 Jul–Aug daily 12–3, 8–11; closed Mon Sep–Jun (except school hols), Jan

LE CROISIC
Le Saint Alys (€–€€)

Small, nautical-themed restaurant at the port. Meat and fish dishes cooked with flair. Try crunchy langoustines with a cider *jus*.

✉ 3 quai Hervé Rielle ☎ 02 40 23 58 40 🕐 Daily 12–2, 7:30–9; closed Sun eve, Tue eve, Wed, Feb

GUÉRANDE

Les Remparts (€€)

Regional cuisine and good seafood in a modern setting at this small hotel-restaurant near the tourist office. The mussels and the duck are always popular choices.

✉ 14–15 boulevard du Nord ☎ 02 40 24 90 69 🕓 Apr–Sep daily 12–1:30; Oct–Mar Tue–Sun; closed Dec to mid-Jan, 1 week Feb, evenings

Roc-Maria (€)

Charming *crêperie* in a 15th-century building within the town walls. Gourmet pancakes such as *La Turballaise* – mussels, prawns and scallops in saffron cream flavoured with *pommeau*.

✉ 1 rue Vieux Marché aux Grains ☎ 02 40 24 90 51 🕓 Tue–Sun 12–10 closed mid-Nov to mid-Dec, Mon Oct–Mar

NANTES

La Cigale (€–€€€)

See page 58.

Le Un (€–€€)

Fashionable, buzzy brasserie on the Île de Nantes. Most dishes have an Eastern influence, like glazed pork with fried noodles.

✉ 1 rue Olympe de Gouges ☎ 02 40 08 28 00; www.leun.fr 🕓 12–3, 7–11

LE POULIGUEN

Café Jules (€–€€)

This stylish bar-restaurant next to the marina. The *café gourmande* – espresso accompanied by mini desserts – is worth the trip.

✉ 15 quai Jules Sandeau ☎ 02 40 42 31 79; www.cafejules.com 🕓 Daily 12:30–2:30, 7–10:30

ST-LYPHARD

Le Nézil (€–€€)

Another typical thatched restaurant in local style offering a fine range of local dishes, including eel, frogs' legs and pike.

✉ St-Lyphard ☎ 02 40 91 41 41 🕓 Daily 12–2, 7:15–9; closed early Oct, mid-Nov to mid-Dec, late Jan–early Feb, Sun eve, Mon, Wed eve Oct–Mar

SHOPPING

Brasserie de la Brière
Classic real ales from a local micro-brewery in a pretty Brière village. Phone beforehand for details of tours and tastings.

✉ Le Nézyl, St-Lyphard ☎ 02 40 91 33 62 🕓 9–12, 2–6:30; closed Sun am

Manuel
This sweet shop on the seafront sells the best ice cream in town. You'll also find chocolates and biscuits.

✉ 2 avenue du Général de Gaulle, La Baule ☎ 02 40 60 20 66

Les Rigolettes Nantaises
Named after the little fruit sweets the owner invented, this old-fashioned shop also sells chocolates, salted-butter caramels and *gâteau nantaise* – sponge cake covered in rum and apricot jam.

✉ 18 rue Verdun, Nantes ☎ 02 40 47 58 31 🕓 Mon–Sat 10–7

ENTERTAINMENT

B'Ollywood
Cinema-themed bar that attracts an older crowd thanks to its retro music. Barman Jerôme makes mean vodka cocktails.

✉ 151 avenue Général de Gaulle, La Baule ☎ 09 51 44 64 51; www.bollywood-bar.fr 🕓 Mon–Fri 6:30pm–1am, until 2am at weekends

La Bouche d'Air
This small venue northwest of the cathedral specializes in staging performances by emerging local, national and international artists from a wide variety of musical genres.

✉ Salle Paul Fort, 9 rue Basse Porte, Nantes ☎ 02 51 72 10 10; www.labouchedair.com 🕓 Box office: Tue–Fri 9–1, 2–6:30

Casino
Sharing premises with the exclusive Marie-Louise hotel, this smart casino offers slot machines and gaming tables.

✉ 24 esplanade Lucien Barrière, La Baule ☎ 02 40 11 48 28; www.lucienbarriere.com 🕓 Gaming tables: Wed–Fri 9pm–3am (until 4am Sat, Sun)

Morbihan

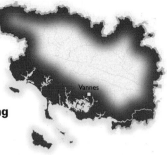

The name Morbihan means 'Little Sea' in Breton, a reference to the *département's* most striking geographical feature. The Golfe du Morbihan, a huge tidal lagoon, is a strange, landlocked maze of muddy creeks and grass-topped islands. In summer, it buzzes with excursion boats and flurrying sails. It's an important over-wintering ground for countless migrant seabirds and wildfowl.

Morbihan's megaliths are world-famous. Carnac's *alignements* (mysterious lines of standing stones) iare one of the region's prime visitor attractions, rivalled by Locmariaquer and the island of Gavrinis, which boasts Brittany's most ornate prehistoric tomb.

The low-lying coastline lacks the drama of the Pink Granite or Emerald coasts, but sheltered sandy beaches and offshore islands, especially Belle-Île, compensate. Exploring the area via the Nantes–Brest Canal offers a new dimension.

AURAY

This ancient place has played a significant role in Breton history. It is now a bustling and sizeable town, and its principal activities include tourism and oyster-raising. Auray is believed to be the last place reached by Julius Caesar in his conquest of Gaul. The Romans established their camp in the river port known today as

St-Goustan, the most picturesque part of the town. Flower-decked, timbered houses and inns surround the quayside place St-Sauveur and the hilly streets near by. The eye-catching schooner moored by the quayside is an old tuna-fishing vessel. Across a quaint 17th-century stone bridge, the church of St-Gildas in the town centre has a fine Renaissance porch. On Auray's northwestern outskirts, shrines and chapels commemorate the martyred members of the Chouan movement led by Georges Cadoudal, who staged an unsuccessful Royalist uprising against Revolutionary forces in 1795.

To the northeast, Ste-Anne-d'Auray is one of Brittany's most important religious sites. A colourful *pardon* on 25 and 26 July attracts pilgrims to its gloomy basilica, built in honour of a 17th-century ploughman's miraculous vision. Of more general interest is the vast war memorial alongside, dedicated to the 250,000 Bretons who perished in the Great War.

www.auray-tourisme.com

🕂 21H 🍴 Le Chasse Marée (€–€€), place St-Sauveur, St-Goustan, 02 97 56 50 46 🚌 Lines 1 (Quiberon–Carnac–Vannes), 6 (Golfe du Morbihan–Vannes) 🚆 Vannes, Quiberon and Lorient (TVG connections to Paris and Quimper) 🚢 Pleasure cruises on the River Auray or to the Golfe du Morbihan

ℹ 20 rue du Lait, Auray, 02 97 24 09 75; 9 rue de Vannes, Ste-Anne-d'Auray, 02 97 57 69 16

BELLE-ÎLE-EN-MER

Brittany's largest island is a popular excursion from Quiberon, near Carnac. Attractive beaches, historic sights and good holiday facilities are the main reasons to venture here. Most people go just for a day-trip and explore the island on a guided coach tour, but Belle-Île's hotels make longer stays feasible (book well ahead).

Ferry passengers land at Le Palais. Above the harbour looms the 16th-century, star-shaped citadelle. A former prison and garrison, it now houses a museum of local history.

Belle-Île's interior consists of a plateau of moorland schist cut by fertile sheltered valleys that protect the white houses from the prevailing wind. The east coast has good safe beaches with watersports facilities; Grandes Sables is the largest and best.

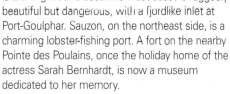

The west coast is ruggedly beautiful but dangerous, with a fjordlike inlet at Port-Goulphar. Sauzon, on the northeast side, is a charming lobster-fishing port. A fort on the nearby Pointe des Poulains, once the holiday home of the actress Sarah Bernhardt, is now a museum dedicated to her memory.

www.belle-ile.com

✚ 20K 🍴 Roz Avel (€€; ➤ 182) 🚌 Taol Mor (Le Palais–Sauzon); excursion buses tour the island 🚢 Boat trips to and from Morbihan's main ports (mainly Quiberon)
ℹ️ Quai Bonelle, Le Palais, 02 97 31 81 93

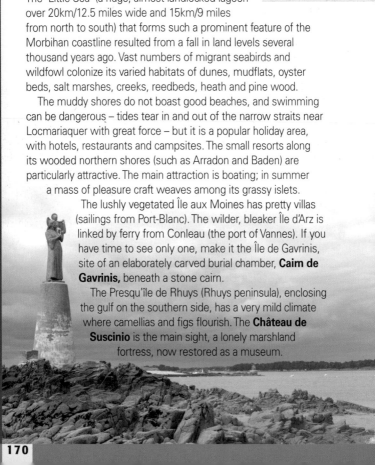

CARNAC
Best places to see, pages 36–37.

GOLFE DU MORBIHAN

The 'Little Sea' (a huge, almost landlocked lagoon over 20km/12.5 miles wide and 15km/9 miles from north to south) that forms such a prominent feature of the Morbihan coastline resulted from a fall in land levels several thousand years ago. Vast numbers of migrant seabirds and wildfowl colonize its varied habitats of dunes, mudflats, oyster beds, salt marshes, creeks, reedbeds, heath and pine wood.

The muddy shores do not boast good beaches, and swimming can be dangerous – tides tear in and out of the narrow straits near Locmariaquer with great force – but it is a popular holiday area, with hotels, restaurants and campsites. The small resorts along its wooded northern shores (such as Arradon and Baden) are particularly attractive. The main attraction is boating; in summer a mass of pleasure craft weaves among its grassy islets.

The lushly vegetated Île aux Moines has pretty villas (sailings from Port-Blanc). The wilder, bleaker Île d'Arz is linked by ferry from Conleau (the port of Vannes). If you have time to see only one, make it the Île de Gavrinis, site of an elaborately carved burial chamber, **Cairn de Gavrinis,** beneath a stone cairn.

The Presqu'île de Rhuys (Rhuys peninsula), enclosing the gulf on the southern side, has a very mild climate where camellias and figs flourish. The **Château de Suscinio** is the main sight, a lonely marshland fortress, now restored as a museum.

www.golfe-du-morbihan.com

✚ 21J

Cairn de Gavrinis

✉ Cale de Pen-Lannic ☎ 02 97 57 19 38; www.gavrinis.info ⏲ Apr–Oct daily for guided tours (reserve ahead) 👆 Expensive (includes ferry) 🛥 Boat trips and entrance tickets from Larmor Baden ☎ 02 97 57 19 38

Château de Suscinio

✉ Kermoizan, Sarzeau ☎ 02 97 41 91 91; www.suscinio.info ⏲ Apr–Sep daily 10–7; reduced hours off season; closed Wed 👆 Moderate

JOSSELIN

The most memorable feature of this medieval town is its mighty fortress, mirrored in the waters of the Oust. The turreted **Château** dates mainly from the 14th century. Its Renaissance façade was added around the turn of the 16th century. The **Musée des Poupées** (doll museum) is in the stable block.

In the town centre, the 12th-century church of Notre-Dame-du-Roncier (Our Lady of the Brambles), contains the tomb of Josselin's erstwhile master, Olivier de Clisson, Constable of France. A *pardon* reveres the patron Virgin. Northeast of Josselin, the Forêt de Paimpont is a popular touring and walking area, mainly for its Arthurian legends. Ploërmel, en route, was the site of a chivalric tournament in 1351, known as the Battle of the Thirty.

www.paysdejosselin-tourisme.com

✚ 10F 🍴 La Table d'O (€–€€; ➤ 182) 🚌 Line 2 (Pontivy–Ploërmel) ℹ Place de la Congrégation, 02 97 22 36 43

Château de Josselin/Musée des Poupées

☎ 02 97 22 36 45; www.chateaujosselin.com ⏲ Mid-Jul to Aug daily 11–6; Apr to mid-Jul 2–6; Sep 2–5:30; Oct Sat, Sun 2–5:30 👆 Moderate–expensive

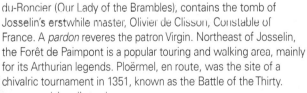

LOCMARIAQUER

This pretty oyster port guarding the neck of the Golfe du Morbihan rivals Carnac in archaeological importance. Its main sights lie in a fenced compound north of the village. They include a huge recumbent menhir, broken into four sections, which would have measured over 20m (65ft) high. Near by is a large decorated dolmen, the **Table des Marchand,** one of several good examples to be seen in the area. In Roman times the town of *Dariorigum* stood on this site, and the Gaullish *Veneti* used it as their naval base. Today, Locmariaquer is a peaceful place with attractive south-facing beaches, a pleasant old harbour quarter and lots of boat trips. Seafront walks from the Pointe de Kerpenhir are excellent.

www.ot-locmariaquer.com

✚ 21H 🍽 Crêperie des Îles (€), 8 place Dariorigum (port) 🚢 Boat trips round Golfe du Morbihan; crossings to Belle-Île and Port-Navalo

ℹ Rue de la Victoire, 02 97 57 33 05

Site des Mégalithes de Locmariaquer

✉ Route de Kerlogonan ☎ 02 97 57 37 59 🕐 Jul–Aug daily 10–7; May–Jun 10–6; Sep–Apr 10–12:30, 2–5:15 ✋ Moderate (combined ticket available for Carnac)

PORT-LOUIS

Port-Louis was named after Louis XIV, under whose reign the town flourished. It avoided the devastating air-raids of World War II

that destroyed much of Lorient, and
retains the air of a modest fishing port.
The fortified citadel at the harbour
entrance was founded in 1591, and later used as a prison, barracks
and arsenal. It now houses a museum complex which includes the
Musée de la Marine (maritime museum) and the **Musée de la
Compagnie des Indes,** dedicated to the history of the East India
Company during the 17th and 18th centuries. Rampart walks give
excellent views of the Lorient roadsteads.

www.ville-portlouis.fr

➕ 19H ⦅🍴⦆ Avel Vor (€€–€€€), 25 route de Locmalo, 02 97 82 47 59

🚌 Line 18 (Carnac) 🚢 Batobus (Lorient)

ℹ 1 rue Citadelle, 02 97 84 78 00

Musée de la Marine/Musée de la Compagnie des Indes

✉ Citadelle de Port-Louis ☎ 02 97 82 56 72 🕐 May to Aug daily 10–6:30;
Sep to mid-Dec, Feb–Apr Wed–Mon 1:30–6 ✋ Moderate

PRESQU'ÎLE DE QUIBERON

A narrow neck of tidal sediment links this feather-shaped peninsula
with the mainland, in places barely wider than the access road
which runs past windswept conifers and dunes of blown sand.
The resort of Quiberon is one of Morbihan's liveliest. As well as
its good sandy beaches and thalassotherapy centre, it is the main

ferry terminal for Belle-Île (➤ 169) and is always
crowded in summer. A sailing school is based in
its sheltered eastern waters. On the west coast,
the Côte Sauvage, the Atlantic beats furiously on
cliffs, crags and caves. The Pointe de Percho offers
good views.

www.quiberon.com

➕ 20J ⦅🍴⦆ Le Vivier (€–€€), Côte Sauvage, 02 97 50 12 60

🚌 Line 1 (Auray–Plouharnel) 🚆 Auray–Vannes 🚢 Frequent
ferries to Belle-Île; also to Houat and Hoëdic islands

ℹ 14 rue de Verdun, 0 825 13 56 00

LA ROCHE-BERNARD

Since the building of the Arzal dam, the Vilaine no longer provides an outlet to the open sea, and pleasure craft are the only boats to reach the town. In past years, however, La Roche-Bernard was a great riverine trading centre, handling cargoes of grain, wine, salt and timber. The **Musée de la Vilaine Maritime,** housed in the Château des Basses-Fosses on the west bank of the river, recounts these prosperous times. Today, the town's revenue comes mainly from tourism. Classed as a *petite cité de charactère*, it makes a most attractive touring base, with an excellent range of restaurants and hotels. The old quarter is packed with charming, flower-decked houses. A graceful suspension bridge spans the river, replacing an earlier version accidentally destroyed when lightning struck a German ammunition base.

www.cc-pays-la-roche-bernard.fr

✚ 23J 🍴 Auberge Bretonne, place Duguesclin (€€–€€€), 02 99 90 60 28

🚌 Lines 8 (Vannes–Nantes), 10 (Redon–Rochefort-en-Terre)

🚢 Boat trips on the Vilaine to Redon and the Arzal dam

ℹ️ 14 rue Dr-Cornudet, 02 99 90 67 98

Musée de la Vilaine Maritime

☎ 02 99 90 83 47 🕐 Mid-Jun to mid-Sep daily 10:30–12:30, 2:30–6:30 ✋ Inexpensive

ROCHEFORT-EN-TERRE

The attractions of this village are very obvious. The setting on a schist spur surrounded by plunging wooded slopes and rushing

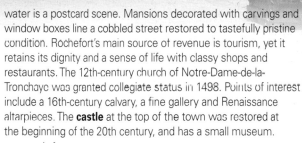

water is a postcard scene. Mansions decorated with carvings and window boxes line a cobbled street restored to tastefully pristine condition. Rochefort's main source of revenue is tourism, yet it retains its dignity and a sense of life with classy shops and restaurants. The 12th-century church of Notre-Dame-de-la-Tronchaye was granted collegiate status in 1498. Points of interest include a 16th-century calvary, a fine gallery and Renaissance altarpieces. The **castle** at the top of the town was restored at the beginning of the 20th century, and has a small museum.

www.rochefort-en-terre.com

✚ 23H 🍴 Le Pélican (€–€€), place des Halles, 02 97 43 38 48 🚌 Lines 9 (Vannes), 10 (Redon)

ℹ Place des Puits, 02 97 43 33 57

Château

☎ 02 97 43 31 56 🕐 Jul–Aug daily 10–6:30; Jun, Sep 2–6:30; Apr, May Sat, Sun 2–6:30 ✋ Moderate

VANNES

This busy commercial centre is one of Brittany's best-looking towns, and more cosmopolitan than most. Its well-preserved old quarter lies behind imposing ramparts, best observed from the promenade de la Garenne, a raised walkway beside colourful public gardens.

Vannes' most picturesque sight, the old *lavoir* (washhouse), stands near the Porte Poterne. The main monument within the walls is the Cathédrale St-Pierre, a hotchpotch of styles from Romanesque to baroque. It houses the tomb of Vannes' patron saint, St Vincent Ferrier. Opposite the cathedral, **La Cohue** is a medieval covered market that once housed the law courts. This building now provides display space for temporary exhibitions and the **Musée des Beaux-Arts,** containing an assortment of Breton paintings. Its star exhibit is Eugène Delacroix's *Crucifixion*.

A wander through Old Vannes reveals many other handsome buildings and squares. The place des Lices, once used for medieval tournaments, holds a produce market every Wednesday and Saturday. Near by are the Maison de Vannes, adorned with quaint carvings of a rustic couple popularly known as Vannes and his Wife, and the Maison de St-Vincent Ferrier.

Vannes is one of southern Brittany's main excursion centres, principally offering boat trips on the Golfe du Morbihan. Pleasure craft moor outside the walled old town, at the *gare maritime* on the Conleau peninsula. The Parc du Golfe here is a leisure park with attractions such as a **butterfly garden** and an **aquarium.**

www.tourisme-vannes.com

🕂 22H 🍴 Le Comptoir (€), 8 rue du Port, 02 97 47 93 38 🚌 TPV local urban services; others run to all main centres in Morbihan 🚆 Redon/Nantes, Auray/Quiberon and Lorient (TGV Paris–Quimper) 🚢 Wide range around Golfe du Morbihan, and to Belle-Île ❓ A *petit train* provides tours of the old town (with commentary)

ℹ Maison du Torisme, quai Tabarly, 0 825 13 56 10

La Cohue/Musée des Beaux-Arts
✉ 9 and 15 place St-Pierre ☎ 02 97 01 63 00 🕐 Mid-Jun to Sep daily 10–6;
off-peak 1:30–6 (public hols) ✋ Moderate (charges vary for temporary
exhibitions)

Le Jardin aux Papillons (butterfly garden)
✉ Parc du Golfe, rue Daniel Gilard ☎ 0 810 40 69 01;
www.jardinauxpapillons.com 🕐 Jul–Aug daily 10–7; Apr–Jun, Sep daily
10–12, 2–6 ✋ Expensive (combined ticket with aquarium available)

Aquarium de Vannes
✉ Parc du Golfe ☎ www.aquarium-du-golfe.com 🕐 Jul, Aug daily 9–7:30;
Apr–Jun, Sep, school hols 10–12, 2–6; Oct–Mar 2–6 ✋ Expensive

a walk around old Vannes

Start this walk from the tourist office on quai Tabarly and head northeast to place Gambetta, just north of the canalized port.

Place Gambetta consists of a terraced crescent of 19th-century buildings, especially lively with cafes and bars in the early evening.

Enter the ramparts via the Porte St-Vincent, and proceed up rue St-Vincent to place des Lices.

The largely pedestrianized streets inside the walls are a relief after the noisy traffic outside. Place des Lices, once a medieval tiltyard, is now the marketplace. Just north of the square, on the corner of rue Noë, stands the quaint Maison de Vannes. Near by is Vannes' history and archaeology museum, in an elegant urban manor called the Château Gaillard. It contains a fine collection of prehistoric objects.

Head northeast to place Valencia.

At No 17 stands the home of St Vincent Ferrier, the town's patron saint, marked by a niched statue.

Head up rue des Orfevres and visit the Cathédrale St-Pierre and La Cohue. Then stroll west from place Henri IV along rue St-Salomon to rue Thiers.

Here are the imposing Hôtel de Limur (a 17th-century town house), and (on place M Marchais) the 19th-century Hôtel de Ville with its fine equestrian statue.

Walk back past the cathedral via rue Burgault and rue des Chanoines. Pass through the machicolated Porte-Prison, then head south past the ramparts along the promenade de la Garenne.

Bright waterside gardens cheer up the stern rampart towers. Notice the picturesque 18th-century *lavoir* (washhouse) by the bridge near Porte Poterne.

Return to place Gambetta and the port, near the start of the walk.

Distance 3km (2 miles)
Time Allow half a day with time for sightseeing
Start point Tourist office (quai Tabarly) 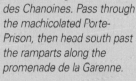 22H
End point Place Gambetta ✚ 18H
Lunch Le Comptoir (€), 8 rue de Port, 02 97 47 93 38

HOTELS

ARRADON
Les Vénêtes (€€€)

A superb waterfront location and stylish decor give this place its special appeal. Smart restaurant with splendid views.

✉ La Pointe ☎ 02 97 44 85 85; www.lesvenetes.com ⊘ Closed two weeks in Jan

AURAY
Le Marin (€–€€)

A charming little bed-and-breakfast hotel quietly tucked behind the historic quayside of St-Goustan. The decor is modern, but the building has quaint old beams.

✉ 1 place du Rolland ☎ 02 97 24 14 58; www.hotel-lemarin.com ⊘ Closed Jan to mid-Feb

BELLE-ÎLE-EN-MER
La Desirade (€€€)

A delightful village-like hotel of low-rise, shuttered buildings set around a swimming pool. Relaxing atmosphere. Relaxing atmosphere and delicious buffet-brunch.

✉ Le Petit Cosquet, Bangor ☎ 02 97 31 70 70; www.hotel-la-desirade.com ⊘ Closed mid-Nov to Mar

CARNAC
Plume Au Vent (€€)

Named after the original comic strips that adorn the walls, this renovated village house offers quiet, TV-free bed-and-breakfast near the megaliths. Breakfast on delicious local fruitbread and jam.

✉ 4 Venelle Notre Dame ☎ 06 16 98 34 79; www.plume-au-vent.com

LA GACILLY
La Grée des Landes (€€–€€€)

Recently opened, eco-friendly hotel and spa owned by Yves Rocher. Enjoy a massage with organic oils before savouring a meal made with local, seasonal produce as you admire the countryside.

✉ Cournon ☎ 02 99 08 50 50; www.lagreedeslandes.com

LOCMARIAQUER
Les Trois Fontaines (€€)
Close to the megaliths, this well-designed, spacious hotel has light, elegant bedrooms, some with sea views. Lovely terrace and flower-filled garden.

✉ Route d'Auray ☎ 02 97 57 42 70; www.hotel-troisfontaines.com
🕐 Closed mid-Nov to Jan

PÉNESTIN
Loscolo (€–€€)
A headland charmer on a quiet, scenic beach near the mouth of the Vilaine. A friendly welcome and great cooking make up for the dated decor.

✉ Pointe de Loscolo ☎ 02 99 90 31 90; www.hotelloscolo.com
🕐 Closed Dec–Mar

LA ROCHE-BERNARD
Auberge des Deux Magots (€)
A pretty, stone-built restaurant-with-rooms on a picturesque old-town square. Empire-style furnishings and good regional cooking.

✉ 1 place du Bouffray ☎ 02 99 90 60 75; www.auberge-les2magots.com
🕐 Closed Christmas, New Year

ST PIERRE QUIBERON
Hotel des Deux Mers (€–€€)
Contemporary furnishings and communicating rooms in a beautiful 1930s beachside house make this the ideal place for fashionable families. Wonderful coastal walks and watersports for the active.

✉ 8 avenue Surcouf, Penthièvre Plage ☎ 02 97 52 33 75; www.hotel-des-deux-mers.com 🕐 Nov–Mar

VANNES
Le Roof (€€–€€€)
A modern hotel in a waterfront setting by the port. Rooms are spacious and comfortable. Take your pick from two restaurants: gourmet and brasserie.

✉ Presqu'île de Conleau ☎ 02 97 63 47 47; www.le-roof.com

RESTAURANTS

BELLE-ÎLE-EN-MER
Roz Avel (€€)

This pretty village house with a pink facade is decorated in 'smart Breton' style. Interesting desserts such as peaches poached in *cassis* accompanied by apricot sorbet. Summer terrace.

✉ Rue du Lieutenant Riau (behind the church), Sauzon ☎ 02 97 31 61 48
🕐 12:15–1:15, 7–9:15; closed mid-Nov to mid-Dec, Jan–late Mar, Wed

CARNAC
La Côte (€–€€)

Family-friendly restaurant in an attractive stone house with a lovely garden terrace. The classic and original dishes include warm Camembert spiced with cumin accompanied by fresh pears.

✉ Alignements de Kermario ☎ 02 97 52 02 80; www.restaurant-la-cote.com
🕐 Daily 12:15–2:15, 7:15–9:15; closed Mon, Tue lunch (Jul, Aug), Sat lunch and Sun eve (Sep–Jun), Jan, 2 weeks Mar, 3 weeks Nov

HENNEBONT
Château de Locguénolé (€€–€€€)

Elegant, extremely grand, riverside hotel with elaborate menus. Fillet of pigeon cooked in black tea with a white asparagus risotto gives a flavour of what's on offer.

✉ Route de Port-Louis ☎ 02 97 76 76 76; www.chateau-de-locguenole.com
🕐 Daily 7:30–9, Sun lunch 12:30–1:30; closed Jan to mid-Feb, Mon Oct–Mar

ÎLE AUX MOINES
Les Embruns (€–€€)

Ten minutes from the landing stage, this blue-and-white restaurant is a reliable choice on one of the gulf's most visited islands.

✉ Rue du Commerce ☎ 02 97 26 30 86 🕐 Mar–Dec Thu–Tue 12–2, 7:30–9

JOSSELIN
La Table d'O (€–€€)

A smart but friendly choice with lovely views over the town and river. Accomplished cooking and good-value lunch menus.

✉ 9 rue Glatinier ☎ 02 97 70 61 39 🕐 Closed Sun eve, Wed Oct–Mar

LORIENT
La Base (€–€€)
Trendy bar-restaurant next to the Cité de la Voile, frequented by sailing stars like Frank Cammas. Scoff a scallop skewer on the waterside terrace and admire the catamarans.

✉ Keroman submarine base ☎ 02 97 88 01 93; www.labaselorient.fr
🕐 Daily 12–3, 7–11

PORT-NAVALO
Le Grand Largue (€€–€€€)
Serves acclaimed fish dishes, such as oysters with seaweed caviar. There's cheaper fare in the brasserie oyster-bar downstairs.

✉ 1 rue du Phare ☎ 02 97 53 71 58 🕐 Daily 12–2, 7:30–9:30; closed Mon, Tue mid-Nov to mid-Feb

QUIBERON
Le Vivier (€–€€)
See page 58.

LA ROCHE-BERNARD
Auberge Bretonne (€€€)
Another leading chef running a celebrated restaurant-with-rooms. Refined service and elegant surroundings. Try something unusual like lobster with pineapple.

✉ 2 place du Guesclin ☎ 02 99 90 60 28 🕐 Daily 12–1:30, 7–8:30; closed mid-Nov to mid-Jan; lunch Wed, Sat, Sun; dinner Thu

LA TRINITÉ-SUR-MER
Le Bistrot du Marin (€–€€)
See page 58.

VANNES
Roscanvec (€–€€€)
Inventive menus, based on what's best at market, in the walled town. Try calves' liver with sweet onion compôte and pancetta.

✉ 17 rue des Halles ☎ 02 97 47 15 96 🕐 Tue–Sat 12:15–2, 7:15–9:30; closed Sun, Mon (except school hols)

SHOPPING

ARTS AND CRAFTS

Le Comptoir Celte

A good place to look for classic Breton products such as woodcarvings, ceramics, boat models and music recordings.

✉ 8 rue St-Vincent, Vannes ☎ 02 97 47 34 03; www.comptoir-celte.fr

🕓 Mon–Fri 10–12:30, 2–6, Sat 10–7

Galerie Plisson

Philip Plisson is a renowned photographer of seascapes, and his gallery includes many memorable Breton scenes.

✉ Mané Lenn, route de la Trinité-sur-Mer ☎ 02 97 30 17 71; www.plisson.com 🕓 Mon–Sat 10–12:30, 2–7, Sun 3–7

Les Poissons de Dilo

Mackerel, mullet and sardines are just some of the fish beautifully reproduced on pieces of driftwood, oars, chests and other maritime finds by the artist Diane Loranchet. Commissions are undertaken.

✉ 18 avenue de Groix, Portivy, St-Pierre-Quiberon ☎ 06 64 31 42 65; www.lespoissonsdedilo.com 🕓 Daily 4–8pm

Yves Rocher

The beauty magnate has turned his home town and production HQ into a tourist attraction, with botanical gardens, a plant museum and an eco-friendly hotel and spa. Naturally the products are on sale.

✉ La Croix des Archers, La Gacilly ☎ 02 99 08 35 55; www.yves-rocher.fr

🕓 Mon–Fri 10–6

FOOD AND DRINK

Maison Lucas

This family-owned smoked fish company offers tastings and 25-minute tours around its factory. Take your pick from wild salmon, eels, herring and more in the on-site shop.

✉ Quai des Saveurs, Z A Plein Ouest, Quiberon ☎ 02 97 50 59 50; www.maisonlucas.net 🕓 May–Sep daily 10–12, 2:15–5:45

Le Rucher Fleuri

Traditional bakery near the main square. Its speciality is *pain d'epices* (spiced bread) in various flavours (nut, raisin, orange etc).
✉ Rue du Porche, Rochefort-en-Terre ☎ 02 97 43 35 78 🕐 11–12:30, 2–6

La Tapenalgue

The best Breton produce such as salted-butter caramels, biscuits and local beers, including the seawater-based Mor Braz.
✉ 23 rue des Halles, Vannes ☎ 02 97 42 69 65 🕐 Jul–Aug daily 9:30–7; closed Sun, Mon am Sep–Jun

La Trinitaine

Many outlets of this large biscuit producer are scattered around Morbihan, but this is one of the largest. Honey, sweets, liqueurs.
✉ Route de Crac'h, St-Philibert, Locmariaquer ☎ 02 97 55 02 04 www.latrinitaine.com 🕐 8:30am–8pm

ENTERTAINMENT

Casino de Carnac

The usual range of slot machines and gaming tables, plus a lively programme of dinner-dancing, disco evenings and other events.
✉ 41 avenue des Salines, Carnac ☎ 02 97 52 64 64; www.lucienbarriere.com 🕐 Gaming tables Sun–Thu 8pm–2am, Fri, Sat 9–3

Chez Mamm Kounifl

Rock, folk and Celtic music take centre stage on Friday and Saturday nights in this well-known cafe-venue between Lorient and Port Louis. Often attracts well-known names.
✉ Route de Port Louis, Locmiquélic ☎ 02 97 33 92 37; www.mamm-kounifl.fr 🕐 Daily 9am–1am

Le Sarah B

Authentic, modern Breton cafe in an old stone house with an arty interior and clientele. Live music from a variety of genres at the weekend; regional produce on the menu.
✉ 9 quai St Antoine, La Roche-Bernard ☎ 02 99 90 74 60; www.lesarahb.fr 🕐 Daily 11:30am–3pm, 6pm–1am, Sat–Sun 11:30am–1am; closed Wed

Index

Acknowledgements

The Automobile Association would like to thank the following photographers, companies and picture libraries for their assistance in the preparation of this book.

Abbreviations for the picture credits are as follows – (t) top; (b) bottom; (c) centre; (l) left; (r) right; (AA) AA World Travel Library.

4l Pontrieux, AA/A Kouprianoff; **4c** Redon, AA/A Kouprianoff; **4r** Quimper, AA/R Strange; **5l** Josselin, AA/A Kouprianoff; **5c** Morlaix, AA/R Strange; **6/7** Pontrieux, AA/A Kouprianoff; **8/9** Carving, St-Thégonnec, AA/A Kouprianoff; **10t** Restaurant, Dinan, AA/A Kouprianoff; **10c** Dinan, AA/A Kouprianoff; **10b** Church, Lampaul, AA/J A Tims; **10/11** Locmariaquer, AA/J A Tims; **11cl** Traditional lace, Quimper, AA/A Kouprianoff; **11cr** Festival dancers, Landerneau, AA/A Kouprianoff; **11b** Domaine de Rochevilaine, Billiers, AA/J A Tims; **12/13** Fresh crabs, AA/A Kouprianoff; **13** Crêpe, AA/B Smith; **14t** La Brasserie des Halles, Vannes, AA/J A Tims; **14b** French bread, AA/A Kouprianoff; **14/15** La Belle Meuniere, St-Cast-le-Guildo, AA/J A Tims; **15tl** Artichokes, AA/R Strange; **15tr** Breton cider, AA/R Strange; **15c** Beers, AA/A Kouprianoff; **16/17t** Crêperie sign, AA/J A Tims; **16c** Brasparts parish close, AA/A Kouprianoff; **16b** Seafood, AA/R Victor; **17t** Pointe de Dinan, AA/R Strange; **17c** Carnac, AA/J A Tims; **17b** Seafood, AA/A Kouprianoff; **18t** Île de Bréhat, AA/P Bennett; **18/19t** Medieval festival, Moncontour, AA/P Kenward; **19l** Beach, Bénodet, AA/R Strange; **19r** Café Breton restaurant, Rennes, AA/J A Tims; **20/21** Redon, AA/A Kouprianoff; **24/25** Bagpipe players, AA/A Kouprianoff; **27** Toll point, outside Calais, AA/J A Tims; **28c** Brest, public transport, AA/J A Tims; **28b** Taxi sign, AA/M Jourdan; **31** Pharmacy sign, AA/J A Tims; **34/35** Quimper, AA/R Strange; **36/37t** Carnac, AA/J A Tims; **36/37b** Carnac, AA/J A Tims; **38/39** Catédrale St-Pierre, Nantes, AA/R Strange; **40/41t** Castle, Fougères, AA/S Day; **40/41b** Castle, Fougères, AA/S Day; **42** Côte de Granit Rose, Penmarc'h, AA/A Kouprianoff; **42/43** Pink granite rocks, near Ploumanac'h, AA/P Bennett; **44t** Castle, Dinan, AA/A Kouprianoff; **44b** Port, Dinan, AA/A Kouprianoff; **44/45** Timber framed shops, Dinan, AA/A Kouprianoff; **46/47** Parish close, Guimiliau, AA/A Kouprianoff; **47t** Gargoyle, Guimiliau, AA/A Kouprianoff; **47b** Carvings, Guimiliau, AA/R Strange; **48/49t & 48/49b** Océanopolis, Brest, AA/A Kouprianoff; **50** Morgat, AA/R Strange; **50/51 & 51** Pointe de Dinan, AA/A Kouprianoff; **52/53** Bridge, Quimper, AA/A Kouprianoff; **53** Café, Quimper, AA/J A Tims; **54/55t** St Malo, AA/S Day; **54/55b** View from St Malo Castle, AA/S Day; **55** Port St Vincent, St-Malo, AA/S Day; **56/57** Josselin, AA/A Kouprianoff; **58/59** Île de Brehat, AA/A Kouprianoff **60/61** Cyclists, Josselin, AA/P Bennett; **62/63t** Lieue de Grève beach, AA/R Strange; **62/63b** Locquirec Bay, AA/A Baker; **64** Traditional lace, Quimper, AA/A Kouprianoff; **66/67** La Baule, AA/R Strange; **68** Branfere Park, Child and Wallaby, Photolibrary Group; **71** Guéhenno, parish close, AA/R Strange; **73** Le Folgoët, AA/R Victor; **74/75** Morlaix, AA/R Strange; **77** Concarneau, AA/A Kouprianoff; **78t** Bénodet, AA/R Strange; **78b** Château and gardens, Brest, AA/A Kouprianoff; **79** Port, Brest, AA/J A Tims; **80/81** Cap Sizun, AA/A Kouprianoff; **82** Pointe du Raz, AA/A Kouprianoff; **83** Cap Sizun, AA/A Kouprianoff; **84/85 & 84** Château de Général Leclerc, AA/A Kouprianoff; **85** Concarneau, AA/A Kouprianoff; **86/87** Île d'Ouessant, coastline, AA/J A Tims; **88** La Place de L'Église, Locronan, AA/P Kenward; **89t** Locronan, Church of St Ronan, AA/R Strange; **89c** Forest of Huelgoat, Monts d'Arrée, AA/R Victor; **90** Morlaix, AA/A Kouprianoff; **90/91** Moulin du Grand Poulguin, Pont-Avent, AA/A Kouprianoff; **91** Gauguin statue, Pont-Aven, AA/A Kouprianoff; **92/93** Parish close, Sizun, AA/R Strange; **93** Kérouat Mills, AA/R Strange; **94t & 94b** Roscoff, AA/A Kouprianoff; **94/95** St-Pol-de-Léon, AA/R Strange; **105** Abbaye de Beauport, AA/P Bennett; **106** Lighthouse, Cap Fréhel, AA/A Kouprianoff; **106/107** Fort de la Latte, AA/S Day; **107** St-Briac-sur-Mer, AA/S Day; **108** Île de Bréhat, AA/A Kouprianoff; **109** Lamballe, AA/A Kouprianoff; **110/111** Place du Général Leclerc, Lannion, AA/R Strange; **111** Port Plaisance, Paimpol, AA/P Bennett; **112/113** Lighthouse, Perros-Guirec, AA/A Kouprianoff; **113** Trégastel beach, AA/P Bennett; **114 & 114/115** Perros-Guirec, AA/A Kouprianoff; **116t** Tréguier, AA/A Kouprianoff; **116b** Tréguier Cathedral, AA/A Kouprianoff; **123** Mont-St-Michel, AA/J Dawson; **124t** Oysters, Cancale, AA/J A Tims; **124b** Château de Combourg, AA/S Day; **124/125** Dinard, AA/S Day; **126t** Mont-Dol, AA/S Day; **126/127** Dol-de-Bretagne, AA/S Day; **127** Castle, Fougères, AA/S Day; **128 & 128/129** Fougères, AA/S Day; **130t & 130c** Hédé, AA/A Baker; **131** Menhir de Champ-Dolent AA/S Day; **132/133** River and boats, Redon, AA/A Kouprianoff; **132** Redon, AA/R Victor; **133** Grand Rue, Redon, AA/A Kouprianoff; **134** St-Pierre church, Rennes, AA/A Kouprianoff; **134/135** Port Mordelaise arch, Rennes, AA/A Kouprianoff; **135** Jardin du Thabor, Rennes, AA/A Kouprianoff; **136/137** Place de Mairie, Rennes, AA/A Kouprianoff; **138 & 138/139** La Roche aux Fées, AA/A Baker; **140/141** Mont-St-Michel, AA/C Sawyer; **142** Tertres Noirs, Vitré, AA/A Kouprianoff; **151** Guérande, AA/R Strange; **152** Batz-sur-Mer, AA/R Strange; **153** La Baule, AA/R Strange; **154** Châteaubriant, AA/R Strange; **154/155** Le Croisic, AA/J Edmanson; **156t** Brière Regional Nature Park, AA/R Strange; **156b** Brière Regional Nature Park, AA/N Setchfield; **157** Brière Regional Nature Park, AA/A Baker; **158/159** Place Royal, Nantes, AA/R Strange; **159** Castle, Nantes, AA/R Victor; **160/161** Palais Dobrée, Nantes, AA/R Strange; **162** Memorial Park, St-Nazaire, AA/J Edmanson; **167** Port-Coton, looking towards Aiguilles, AA/A Kouprianoff; **168** Ste-Anne d'Auray, AA/R Strange; **168/169** Pointe des Poulains, Belle-Île, AA/A Kouprianoff; **169** Suazon, Belle-Île, AA/A Kouprianoff; **170/171t** Locmariaquer, AA/J A Tims; **170/171b** Locmariaquer, AA/J A Tims; **172t** Château, Josselin, AA/P Bennett; **172b** Dolmen des Pierres Plates, Locmariaquer, AA/R Victor; **172/173** Point du Percho beach, Presqu'île de Quiberon, AA/A Kouprianoff; **173** Port-Louis, AA/R Strange; **174** La Roche-Bernard, AA/R Strange; **174/175** Rochefort-en-Terre, AA/A Kouprianoff; **176** Garden, Vannes, AA/J A Tims; **1 76/177** Hôtel de Ville, Vannes, AA/A Kouprianoff; **178/179** Cathedral, Vannes, AA/A Kouprianoff

Every effort has been made to trace the copyright holders, and we apologise in advance for any accidental errors. We would be happy to apply the corrections in the following edition of this publication.

Sight Locator Index

This index relates to the maps on the cover. We have given map references to the main sights in the book. Some sights within towns may not be plotted on the maps.